More Back-Road
4X4 TRIPS

MARIËLLE RENSSEN

First edition published in 2012
by MapStudio™ South Africa

ISBN 978-1-77026-418-2 (Print)
ISBN 978-1-77026-416-8 (ePub)
ISBN 978-1-77026-417-5 (PDF)

Production Manager John Loubser
Project Manager Genené Hart
Editor Thea Grobbelaar
Designer Nicole Bannister
Cartographer Genené Hart
Digital Compiler Anthony Davids
Proofreader Roelien Theron
Reproduction Resolution Colours (Pty) Ltd, Cape Town
Marketing marketing@mapstudio.co.za
Feedback research@mapstudio.co.za
Terrain background for maps kindly supplied by the Peace Parks Foundation
Photo credits © 2012 All images Hirsh Aronowitz and Keith Titley
Printed and bound by CTP Book Printers, Cape Town, South Africa

MapStudio™
Wembley Square, First Floor,
Solan Road, Cape Town
PO Box 1144, Cape Town, 8000
Tel: 0860 10 50 50

www.mapstudio.co.za

Text © 2012 Mariëlle Renssen
Maps © 2012 MapStudio™
© MapStudio™ 2012

The information contained herein is derived from a variety of sources. While every effort has been made to verify the information contained in such sources, the publisher assumes no responsibility for inconsistencies or inaccuracies in the data nor liability for any damages of any type arising from errors or omissions. Reproduction or recording of any maps, text, photographs, illustrations, or other material contained in this publication in any manner including, without limitation, by photocopying and electronic storage and retrieval, is prohibited.

QUICKFINDER

|Ai-|Ais/Richtersveld Transfrontier Park	46
Addo Elephant NP	12
Addo town	7
Afsaal EcoTrail	38
Akkedis Pass	48
Bakkers Pass	81
Barkly Pass	91
Barra Peninsula	147
Bastervoetpad Pass	91
Beaufort West	34
Bedrogfontein 4x4 Trail	10
Berlin Falls	66
Bourke's Luck Potholes	66
Brandvlei	33
Calitzdorp	28
Calvinia	33
Camdeboo NP	20
Caracal Ecotrail	44
Carlisleshoek Pass	93
Carnarvon	34
Chidenguele	140
Eastern Cape	84
Eksteenfontein	53
Elandshoogte Pass	92
Gannaga Pass	31
God's Window	66
Graaff-Reinet	18
Graskop	62
Greater Limpopo Transfrontier Park	139
Helskloof Pass	54
Inhassoro	145
Izintaba Private Game Reserve	79
Jouberts' Pass	88
Juriesdam 4x4 Trail	18
Kamieskroon	44
Karoo NP	24
Kgalagadi Transfrontier Park	108
Komsberg Pass	30
Kraai River Pass	89
Kruger NP	122
Lady Grey	88
Lesotho	96
Lisbon Falls	66
Loeriesfontein	33
Louis Trichardt (Makhado)	72
Loxton	34
Lundean's Nek	95
Mac Mac Falls	66
Mac Mac Forest Retreat	62
Mac Mac Summit Route	64
Maletsunyane Falls	105
Mapungubwe Cultural Tour	76
Mapungubwe NP	72
Marakele NP	80
Massingir Dam	138
Mbombela	62
Mokala NP	83
Motlatse Canyon Panorama Route	58
Mountain Zebra NP	18
Mozambique	134
Namakwa Eco Trail	57
Namaqua NP	44
Naudé's Nek	92
Nieu-Bethesda	19
Noorspoort Pass	21
Nuweveld EcoTrail	38
Otto du Plessis Pass	90
Ouberg Pass	30
Oudeberg Pass	21
Pilgrim's Rest	65
Pofadder	57
Pomene	143
Potlekkertjie Loop	36
Potrivier Pass	92
Rhodes	93
Rooinek Pass	29
Sendelingsdrif	46
Seweweekspoort	28
Soebatsfontein 4x4 Route	45
Somerset East	17
Sonnenrust 4x4 Trail	19
Springbok	45
Steytlerville	22
Sundowner Route	106
Sutherland	28
Swaershoek Pass	16
Tankwa Karoo NP	28
Tofo	140
Tshugulu Eco Trail	77
Vilanculos	145
Vioolsdrif	55
Volunteershoek Pass	94
Wartrail Valley	94
Waterberg Meander	80
Wepener	107
Wildeperdehoek Pass	45
Willowmore	22
Zastron	100
Zuurberg Pass	16

"VISION – Peace Parks Foundation envisages the establishment of a network of protected areas that links ecosystems across international borders. Given the proximity of the region's protected areas to each other, the possibility exists to create wildlife dispersal routes between them or in certain instances link them. MISSION – Peace Parks Foundation facilitates the establishment of transfrontier conservation areas (peace parks)" and develops human resources, thereby supporting sustainable economic development, the conservation of biodiversity and regional peace and stability. Our GIS Programme now in its 10th year has offered mapped visual support to the various countries and agencies' planning, decision making and management structures across the full network of these southern African protected areas. Please visit www.peaceparks.org for more detailed information"

Contents

Quickfinder	2
Introduction	4
Addo Elephant NP, Mountain Zebra NP, Camdeboo NP	6
Tankwa Karoo NP, Karoo NP	24
Namaqua NP, |Ai-|Ais/Richtersveld Transfrontier Park	40
Mac Mac Summit Route, Motlatse Canyon Panorama Route	58
Mapungubwe NP, Waterberg Meander, Marakele NP	68
Eastern Cape – 11 mountain passes in 3 days	84
West-central Lesotho	96
Kgalagadi's wilderness camps	108
Back-roads Kruger	122
Southern-central Mozambique	134
Southern Africa Road Atlas	150
Packing list	157
Tourist resources	158

Introduction

Our hope is that, with you holding this book right now, you already know us – and our philosophies – from our first book, *Our Top 4x4 Trips*. We had such fun doing it, and clearly so many of you off-road enthusiasts had just as much fun reading it, that we decided to do it all over again. So we've just completed the immensely tough job (twist my arm, twist my arm!) of exploring South Africa – and Mozambique – to bring you our insights and share our experiences. We'd like to prise you off that tar … get you back onto gravel and stones and sand. And we trust that the maps, words and pictures in this, our second book, will inspire you to do just that. This book, with its 10 new trips, presents a launch pad for your own back-road adventures, to be moulded and adapted entirely to suit *you*.

Having bumped and swayed across tens of thousands of kilometres, though, our philosophy and basic rules remain the same. We value our comforts! Camping just isn't in our blood. Hey, if you want to camp, by all means do so. But there's no sage advice from us on that front. For everything else, we try our best: the roads we

expressly chose, those we avoided, what we loved en route, what stuck in our gullet, our brilliant moves, our mistakes, what we got wrong and what we got really, really right (and believe me, we got better and better each time).

We still make a good team. Keith and Hirsh research and plot, consult maps and devise new routes. They also take all the photographs. In the kitchen, I (wisely) keep my hands bound and tied while Hirsh, egged on by Keith (variety, variety!), produces ever more inspired meals. Which leaves me to do the writing: best, and hardest, job of all. Uh … and when it comes to a sucking-mud rescue, Keith has proved his mettle with his calm practicality – and his Toyota Hilux.

Passion plays a big part in our book. We're passionate about what we do, about our country, Africa, the wilds, nature. I could be deemed a little over-enthusiastic with my lists – birds, plants, trees, geology – but that's simply to satisfy an enquiring mind. Hopefully you have one too. The more keenly you observe the natural world surrounding you, the more meaningful it becomes. It's like bird-watching. Once you start trying to identify, say, a particularly striking tree – its crusty bark, moon-shaped pods, pom-pom sprays or star-shaped leaves – it becomes an addiction. Try it, you'll see. (Useless to do this without an armful of books and identification guides, though.)

What needs to be said – and this is important – is that, having no school-going children to speak of, Keith, Hirsh and I have had the luxury of always planning our trips way outside high season and school holidays. This brings with it exclusivity and perfect solitude. More times than we can count ours have been the only two vehicles on the road. We've also been given the pick of the chalets, suites or bungalows, and have had entire lodges to ourselves, which resulted in very specific experiences. (Of course, you might love crowded, traffic-choked, rowdy hilarity. Some do.) That said, we have discovered that foreign travellers are filing into the country like an infantry, especially in their July/August summer break.

In the end, our experience may not end up being yours, and you may choose to arrange your own trip quite differently. But our intention is to steer you in the right direction, guide you through the pitfalls and, always, let you learn from our experience. In fact, we've got so hooked on doing this, we've turned it into a business! (*Visit: Back Road Tours www.backroadtours.co.za*)

Now it simply remains for you to programme your GPS, let down your tyres and head for that soft sand …

Our non-negotiables

Hot shower
There's only so much roughing it this girl and two boys can take. Shivering under the needle-sharp blast of a cold shower doesn't make the cut. Four walls and a solid roof over our heads, water that runs hot in the taps – that does us just fine, thanks.

Flush toilets
Hey, this is the 21st century. Outhouses and long drops are for Neanderthals. Even the fishing camp at Massingir Dam in Mozambique had water-filled cisterns. A flushing loo is not that hard to find …

Cold beers
Dust-coated lungs and a long, hard day's wrestling with a steering wheel – it takes something wet and frosty to wash all that soil down. A chalet that comes with a fridge, then, is a no-brainer. It also does a good job of supplying ice for our cool boxes.

Acknowledgements

We are indebted to **Tracks4Africa** for navigational software that always provides accurate and up-to-date coverage of obscure tracks and off-road routes. This has saved us more than once.

While negotiating the gravel back roads, our **Zartek** two-way radios facilitated clear communication over distances of up to 3km — the lead vehicle could warn of road conditions and any travel hazards ahead, and announce potential scenic spots for our much-needed coffee breaks.

Sand, ruts, mud, stones – our All Terrain **Yokohama** tyres handled them all without a single puncture … anytime … anywhere.

Addo Elephant NP, Mountain Zebra NP, Camdeboo NP

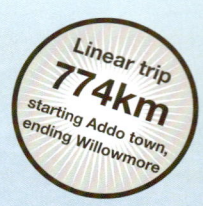

Linear trip 774km starting Addo town, ending Willowmore

What's so special about this route?

Our intention: To explore some of the byways and back roads of the Eastern Cape and Karoo, instigated by a handful of recently established national-park 4x4 trails, one being Addo's new 45km Bedrogfontein trail. Although not all technically challenging, these trails did invite us into undeveloped territory not generally open to the public. And the gravel back roads surprised us with awe-inspiring scenery.

Trip summary

Features: Mountain passes, 4x4 trails (Grade 2), gravel back roads, panoramic scenery
Trip duration: 8 days, 774km
Time of year: End of July (midwinter)
Linear trip: Addo town to Willowmore
Road conditions: Muddy, rutted, stony gravel roads; steep bouldered ascents/descents in 4x4 section

Getting there (Addo town)

From Johannesburg: N1 to Colesberg, N9 to Middelburg, N10 to Paterson, R342 to Addo town
From Durban: N2 to Colchester, R342 to Addo town
From Port Elizabeth: N2, R102, R335 to Addo town
From Cape Town: N2, R334 (via Uitenhage), R342 to Addo town

MORE INFORMATION: **Plan Your Trip Info: page 23**
Tourist Resources: pages 158–160
MAPS: **This Route's Map: pages 8–9**
Also in Road Atlas Section: pages 150–156

Bedrogfontein 4x4 Trail, Addo NP (45km)
Day 1: Kirkwood to Kabouga Cottage
(2x4; Grade 1–2; 2 hours)

This trail runs between the Kabouga and Darlington sections in Addo's north-western reaches. You enter the park, via Kirkwood, through the ranger's gate where permits are checked.

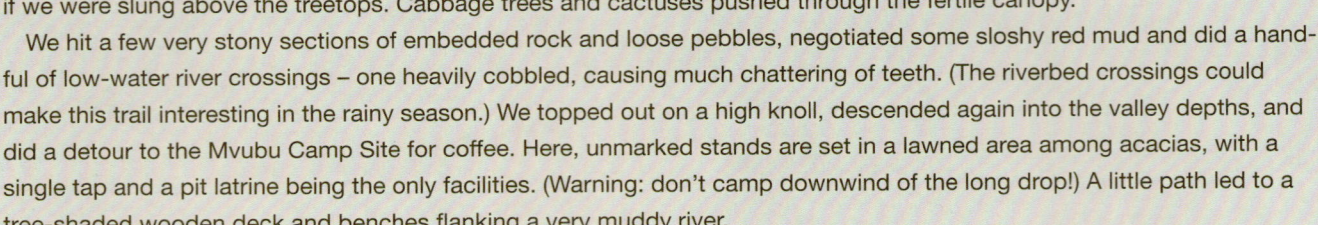

Our plan was to cover the trail in two sections, overnighting in Kabouga Cottage (in fact, a house), and we returned to Addo to do it independently. The first day, from Kirkwood to the house, is suitable for 2x4 vehicles.

At the time, Michael was on duty – a character with a great sense of humour, his dialogue liberally peppered with 'nice and lovely'. We started on quite well-maintained gravel. Sandwiched between banked wooded slopes, our 4x4s meandered up high hills and dipped sharply into deep valleys. Sunshine-yellow sweet-thorns① hugged the road tightly; at times it seemed as if we were slung above the treetops. Cabbage trees and cactuses pushed through the fertile canopy.

We hit a few very stony sections of embedded rock and loose pebbles, negotiated some sloshy red mud and did a handful of low-water river crossings – one heavily cobbled, causing much chattering of teeth. (The riverbed crossings could make this trail interesting in the rainy season.) We topped out on a high knoll, descended again into the valley depths, and did a detour to the Mvubu Camp Site for coffee. Here, unmarked stands are set in a lawned area among acacias, with a single tap and a pit latrine being the only facilities. (Warning: don't camp downwind of the long drop!) A little path led to a tree-shaded wooden deck and benches flanking a very muddy river.

Then we took the short Kabouga Loop before heading to the house. A tight, tree-fringed road marked by humps, bumps and stones twisted along the foot of upended rock cliffs. We'd seen kudu, tippy-toed ostriches and a Hamerkop, while Steppe, Forest and Jackal Buzzards and a Booted Eagle all had made us linger.

In the late afternoon (in January it was still frightfully hot – 37°C at 16:00!), an hour-long drive on the 2x4 Woodlands Loop had us threading through wooded valleys with stony stretches, steep descents and pebbled (dry) riverbeds. The road wasn't particularly challenging, but red soils and deep congealed mud tracks foretold a different story under wet conditions. We marvelled at the prolific blue plumbago covering entire hillsides and the air shimmied with tiny white butterflies. The track rose suddenly and we were at the top of a mount. This was followed by a series of hill crests, then down we went into the valley again. This time we spotted red hartebeest (and babies), grysbok and duiker, and watched Fork-tailed Drongos dive-bombing an African Harrier Hawk.

Kabouga Cottage is a plain, flat-roofed, steel-windowed house sitting at the base of rock cliffs. It has a narrow verandah with a wooden table and benches, an open kitchen/lounge, two bedrooms and a bathroom. Nearby, under tall trees, is a concrete-walled circular lapa and benches.

Day 2: Kabouga Cottage to Darlington Dam
(4x4; Grade 1–3; 4 hours excluding optional Grade 5 river crossing)

We set out on our second leg in mist and drizzle after deflating our tyres to 1.7 bars, in anticipation of wet and muddy roads. The trail started benignly enough through dense woodland on a stony, humpy, winding road.② This time there were gulleys and washaways as we climbed steep inclines that afforded marvellous views of interwoven green hills. Sometimes narrow, twisting and tightly hemmed in, sometimes immensely bouldered and rocky (high clearance is essential), the road climbed and dipped, then turned on itself, all the while hugging the mountain edge. We bumped and bounced past giant cycads and remnants of windmills. The scariest stretch was a deeply angled upward slope riddled with holes and vicious humps – again, high clearance and low range are required. Climbing, climbing, a ribbon of track cut into the mountain with vertiginous drops into a valley 300m below – and no road barriers. You don't want to make a wrong move here. We crested at 340m, from where you could see the road descending and then snaking over the next hill.

Suddenly, at 400m, a sign loomed ahead, marking the 'start' of the Darlington 4x4 Trail (a.k.a. Bedrogfontein). We'd just accomplished quite a hairy 10km in 1½ hours! This could be interesting, we thought. But after much of the same – tracking the mountain edge, diving into tightly vegetated valleys,③ crossing (dry) pebbled riverbeds, boulder-hopping very long rocky stretches – we were a little bemused. Although it required slow careful navigation, the worst had been tackled, we felt. Next, from a magical forest of lichen-encrusted trunks, tangled lianas and draped old man's beard – highly atmospheric in the rain – we looped up and along mountain contours to 860m, where we passed through a rock portal. Darlington Dam lay like a giant pale, streaky cloud on the horizon; a series of hairpin bends wound back and forth below us. Dropping very quickly through 200m, we saw a lone gemsbok, mountain reedbuck and a few kudu, then cruised across a flat valley through Darlington's Nama Karoo vegetation, marked by vygies, euphorbias and other succulents, to Darlington Dam.

We avoided the Grade 5 river loop (from Kabouga over the Langrugkloof) – but that's your call … You could be braver than we are.

DAY 1
Addo town to Addo Elephant NP Main Camp (14.5km)
Leg time without stops: 15 minutes

Although this trip officially starts from the tiny town of Addo, we left in the early morning from Knysna via Uitenhage. The signs all proclaimed it to be a 'water-stressed' area – but that, patently, was then. And this was now. (Thank you, REM!) Heaven's angelic creatures were having fun overturning buckets of rain onto our vehicles. Trees and bushes knee-deep in water, drowned fields, muddy water crashing over bridges, zigzag channels cut into road verges by the rain … it was just the right kind of mud our all-terrain tyres were yearning for after having been mothballed for three years while Hirsh and I entertained adventures of a more urban kind in the Big Apple. In the interim, Keith stopped talking to us.

But we're back – and on speaking terms again. And hungry for potholes and corrugations and a prize-worthy coating of dust to mar the purity of our white vehicle-paintwork.④

And well, yes, Addo could be seen to be a tad tame for a proper off-road jaunt, but it was a way to stub our toes against the rough after so much glass and concrete. And our plan was to spend time in the wilder, less developed southern part of the park.

So here we were, taking the back roads, sloshing through wooded green hills where bitter aloes⑥ and red-hot poker-like Cape speckled aloes, tree euphorbias and agaves – their dried-out, untidy spears listing – made it clear we were in the Eastern Cape.

☨ NORTHEAST ON R342 FROM ADDO TOWN ON TAR (12.6KM), TURN RIGHT TO ADDO NP ENTRANCE (2KM)

Despite the waterlogged potholes and unsolicited car-wash-style deluges from passing trucks, the boys were in good spirits. They passed the time testing out their short-range Zartek radios, plotting ways to deal with me when I got unruly. 'We'll strap Madame to the roof in her favourite camping chair, the one that has a little holder for her beer,' Keith began. 'We'll even give her a little parasol for the rain. Good sport, your missus.'

Loud hilarity at both ends of the radio.

Whatever it takes to keep them focused on the road …

A troop of impala huddled disconsolately in the rain, juxtaposed with sheep and citrus orchards. Ironical to have oranges and grapefruits on the borders of Addo; you're not permitted to carry any citrus fruits in the park. You'll have an elephant's trunk probing past your nostrils faster than you can accelerate.

After signing in at Addo Main Camp's reception, we off-loaded at our two thatched cottages, designed in Cape vernacular style⑦ and sitting among shiny lime-green *spekboom* trees on a hill slope overlooking a valley with a water hole some distance away. It was time for some game-viewing. Because it was mid-afternoon, we set off to do a couple of loops not too far from the camp: Gorah and Rooidam.

A pair of motley, weather-scoured elephant skulls, looking like giant monkey faces, were a leery start as we slowly cruised through an endlessly green landscape of low, tightly packed, small-leaved bushes festooned in mosses and lichens. It was like a magical forest for tiny tots. This was broken by great sweeps of grassland and denuded sweet-thorn acacias bristling with sharply honed, giant white needles. How these thorns are considered to be 'sweet' defies all logic.

SANParks claims that there are over 500 elephant in the park, so we were expecting regular encounters with bulky herds of pachyderms. We had to look hard. There were Burchell's zebra with a baby in the herd whose head seemed out of proportion to its tiny body; prolific warthog with the meanest tusks I've ever seen; a male kudu with stately curlicue horns; a black-backed jackal hidden in the grasses; and finally a couple of lone bull elephants⑤ with red dusty backs, snatching at sweet grass and funnelling it into their mouths. There were also ostriches and herons and hadedas. Common Fiscals, their luminous white chests visible on just about every second tree, ruled the realm. We spotted beautiful African Hoopoes, Black-shouldered Kites and – great excitement! – an African Harrier Hawk with its distinctive yellow face mask. And, as we turned for home, two small family groups of elephant glided through the bush, trailed by a pair of babies testing out their little trunks. So they *were* around, after all …

As we braaied in fine misting rain, we decided we liked having to look a little harder for our wildlife; it dispelled the wrongful myths in our heads that Addo might be a bit of an elephant zoo (our trip blasted that myth out of the sky). That night our dreams were interrupted by the howling of black-backed jackal and the whinnying of spotted hyena. Ah, New York can't compete. Africa doesn't come better than this.

> *… even too cold for bat-eared foxes in their earmuffs*

DAY 2
Addo Main Camp to Matyholweni Camp (38km excluding game-viewing loops)
Leg time without stops: 1 hour

Even the severe Eastern Cape winter (padded jacket, beanie, scarf and gloves required) didn't deter us from believing that the animals roll out of bed early. So, heavily bundled up, teeth chattering, we set off at an ungodly hour to find lion. Because we were going to overnight in the southern part of Addo, we stuck to the loops sandwiched between Main Camp and the road that uncomfortably slices the central section of this massive park in two. Forget the king of beasts. There was *niks*, *nada*, *niente*. Of *anything*. 'What time do they let the animals out of their cages?' Hirsh asked into the radio. 'It's a public holiday,' came Keith's reply.

What we did have, though, was surround-sound bird song that piped, warbled, trilled and tweeted around us (*see* panel, this page). And the scenery was beautiful: at times, from our elevated perspective, we looked onto a jade-green canopy of treetops rolling out to every horizon. We could spy slivers of water and ribbon-roads winding away from us, as a puffy layer of cloud hung in the valley.

We should have known the animals would still be tucked under their duvets. 'It's even too cold for bat-eared foxes in their earmuffs,' quipped Hirsh.

Spotted (Addo NP)
Bokmakierie
Malachite Sunbird
Brown-hooded Kingfisher ⑧
Fiscal Flycatcher
Fork-tailed Drongo
Sombre Greenbul
Lark-like Bunting
Cardinal Woodpecker
Southern Boubou
White-backed Mousebird
Spotted Thick-knee (Dikkop)
Southern Black Korhaan

SANParks check list
All SANParks chalets are equipped with:
♦ Small soaps
♦ Towels
♦ Dishwashing liquid
♦ Kitchen cloths
♦ Basic pots and pans
♦ Cutting board
♦ Crockery
♦ Cutlery
♦ Fridge, stove, microwave, kettle

Note: Rondavels with communal kitchen: **no kettle**

The excitement then ratcheted up a notch. We were driving southward through the park to the Colchester Section, heading for Matyholweni Camp at the southernmost border, when we turned a corner and were confronted by a troop of elephants. Headed up by a posse of females herding a host of young ones, with a bull bringing up the rear, they marched purposefully towards us. We stopped, idling quietly to assess the situation, but they didn't miss a beat. A wary tusked matriarch strode out towards our 4x4 – Hirsh and I had the dubious honour of having front-row seats – and planted herself firmly in front of our bumper. By now we'd cut the engine and were sitting stock-still, hardly breathing as her trunk probed and waved over the bonnet. Sensing no movement, she lumbered quietly by Hirsh's window⑩ and then past Keith's.

It didn't quite end there. A second female, trunk outstretched and looking a little more threatening, bore down on us as the rest of the troop herded the littlies off into the bush, stage left. At this point my heart was playing a bongo solo in my chest and I'd stopped breathing. She hesitated momentarily, suddenly switching to the right, passing so close to me that she almost brushed my window. I made out every wrinkle and fold of her wizened hide. Her eyes wavered as she went past me. Then she was gone, melting into the trees, along with the rest of her family.

With the release of tension, I dissolved into hysterical laughter. For a while we couldn't speak but just gazed at each other wordlessly. Addo a zoo? Never.

As we wound our way south, we digressed onto the various game-viewing loops, struck by the changes to the terrain. It was more mountainous and thickly forested, with sizeable trees, quite unlike the stunted bush of the north. We climbed crests with high vistas over the landscape, then descended to a tight, deep valley lined with otherworldly tree euphorbias, like something out of a science fiction movie. Entire hillsides were covered in cactuses. Glossy Fork-tailed Drongos were vying with Common Fiscals for territorial supremacy.

In-between were yellowed grasslands where the plains game hung out: Burchell's zebra, red hartebeest, lots of curve-tusked warthog, vervet monkeys – and our first Secretary Bird, quill feathers arching.

We inched our way behind a dusty bull elephant on a very slow, leisurely amble along the road ahead. Just as we were becoming impatient with this forced go-slow, he wheeled round, trunk raised, then stopped. The Golf sedan in front of us furiously back-pedalled to a safer distance. The bull looked long and hard at us, irritated by the three vehicles on his tail, then trundled into the bush.

Next: jubilation at our first sighting of buffalo, which had seemed pretty scarce.⑪ A very old bull was quietly seated in a clearing as if waiting to die. This sighting was followed by two males with enormous bosses, then six or seven males, a couple of which were vigorously thrashing and grinding their horns, with expressions of pure ecstasy, against low tree branches. A pair locked horns in a show of male dominance.

Nearing our destination, we felt quite replete. With some patience it had, after all, been a very fruitful day. We crested a rise to find a small

Conspicuous Addo vegetation
Cape speckled aloe (*Aloe microstigma*)
Krans aloe (*Aloe arborescens*)
Uitenhage aloe (*Aloe africana*)
Tick-berry bush (*Chrysanthemoides monilifera*)
Spekboom / Pork bush (*Portulacaria afra*)
Ghwarrie (*Euclea undulata*)
Karoo boer-bean (*Schotia afra*)
Crossberry (*Grewia occidentalis*)
Climbing milk bush (*Euphorbia* sp.)
Leafless worm (*Cadaba aphylla*)
Common *taaibos* (*Rhus pyroides*)
Karee and Currant (*Rhus* spp.)
Sosatie bush (*Crassula rupestris*)
Tree euphorbia (*Euphorbia triangularis*)⑨

⑩

Gauteng sedan reversing urgently towards us. The driver pulled up alongside us and in a voice tinged with fear said, 'He's not so happy, this one … very aggressive … he's got a bad temper.' He then reversed further till the car was safely installed behind Keith.

Great. In the firing line again.

Stomping up the road was a bull elephant, trunk flailing, head waving from side to side. We rolled up our windows and cut the engine. At this point we didn't want *anything* further to raise his ire. Lodged in-between two vehicles, we couldn't make a getaway either way! I had visions of him angrily pushing our Freelander onto its side with us helplessly rolling around on the roof. We've all heard the stories. He thundered towards us, tail whipping, then, as he approached us, suddenly changed course and veered past Hirsh, who was sitting frozen, staring straight ahead, not daring to meet the bull's gaze. The elephant barrelled past Keith and the Gauteng car and headed down the road we'd come.

I was hyperventilating, my heart thumping so loud in my ears that it obliterated the sound of Hirsh's voice next to me.

Enough already. Too much excitement for one day.

DAY 3

Matyholweni Camp to Main Camp (38km excluding viewing loops)
Leg time without stops: 1 hour

We loved our chalets at Matyholweni (Xhosa for 'in the bush' – and that's exactly how it felt). With pitched roofs, wooden beams, clay floor tiles and wooden decks with *rietdak* ceilings in front, the chalets were tucked into dense bush thicket in such a way that made them all private. Most SANParks chalets are decorated in ethnic style, with woven baskets and framed drawings of African masks, together with cushions and bedspreads in earthy, ethnic designs. And it works. But these were just a little nicer, with beds facing glass doors that opened onto vegetation-framed decks.

Be warned, though. Matyholweni's position near Colchester, at the Sundays River mouth, is a handful of kilometres off the N2 highway, so with the traffic sounds at night, you don't particularly feel that you're in the wild. But other than the chalet zone, there are no fences – not even around the reception area – so you're advised not to walk around or get out of your car at any time (six lion having recently been introduced to the park).

Today (again) we were on the prowl for lion. We'd been told this

> **... sitting frozen, staring straight ahead, not daring to meet the bull's gaze.**

was a good part of the park to see them, particularly around the Ndlovu area and on the Mbotyi Loop. Even though lion are generally spotted early or late in the day, we were sure no self-respecting lion would emerge before 07:30, particularly since it was -2°C when we set off.

Heading for the Ndlovu Lookout, we got to see in the far distance the blue ribbon of the Indian Ocean, bleached sand dunes – and the highway to Port Elizabeth! Mightily incongruous. This was the Woody Cape section of Addo, best for hiking trails and bird-watching. But we were on a different mission.

The animals, we noticed, were a lot more skittish than those up north – the presence of predators (lion, spotted hyena), no doubt. But beyond the usual kudu, warthog and two elephants with a pair of babies, the lion were elusive. The bird life, on the other hand, was good: Crowned Hornbill, Brown-hooded Kingfisher, Black-shouldered Kite, Rock Kestrel and juvenile Jackal Buzzard. And, wonder of wonders, a smallish long-legged bird with a yellow chest and neon-orange throat mewing on a sand berm: an Orange-throated Longclaw! First time ever … we were ecstatic.

We drove on through thickly forested hills with cactuses entangled in creepers, tall orange-headed Uitenhage aloes thrusting through the canopy, and trees encrusted with lichens and draped in old man's beard.

Then we were back in Addo's northern section; it was time for coffee at Jack's Picnic Site. We'd found this fenced-in 'botanical reserve' the day before and liked its spotless ablution facilities and secluded tables and benches nestled in the thicket. Here the fenced vegetation is compared with the vegetation in the park to see how herbivores, such as elephant, affect the plant life. (Jack was a black rhino that was part of the park's conservation programme, just in case you want to know.)

What did catch our eye at Jack's was a map of the park with coloured magnets used to indicate what animals had been spotted each day by visitors. And there it was: a red square placed on a spot called Carol's Rest. Lion! The hunt was on.

It took us a while, female elephant and her two babies notwithstanding, to get to the Gorah Loop where the Carol's Rest water hole revealed nothing. We were now on a vast grassland plateau and continued climbing, eyes desperately scanning the grasses for any signs. We should have known to look for the mass convergence of cars. The town crier must have done his rounds because there were about ten vehicles – buses, park jeeps, 4x4s, Citi Golfs (how do they do it?!) – at the crest of the plateau, radiating out from the edge of the road. Having strained my eyes for days peering into all the secret pathways that snaked into dense tangled thicket, I was certain this was where they were hiding (where does 'lion's den' come from, after all?). But here they lay, two very replete lion a couple of metres from the road, on the largest, flattest, most open grass plain imaginable … in the middle of the day. A mangled, gorged-on antelope carcass lay some metres off. And, despite the paparazzi hoopla, the pair was utterly unconcerned.

The male, supple and rippled and shiny, with a gorgeous orange-brown mane, was lying stretched out, hind leg in the air. Nothing does relaxation better than a cat. The sleepy, heavy-lidded female (her tracking collar spoiled the scene somewhat) slowly roused herself, padded a couple of metres and flopped down again. Click-click went the cameras. We were entranced.

After a good half-hour's worth of voyeurism, the rumbling in our stomachs was not to be ignored. 'Ready for lunch?' Hirsh asked into the radio. 'My Skippy's ready to jump out of the storage box,' came Keith's voice.

So back to Addo Main Camp it was, this time to thatched rondavels. Although tiny, the units – each with a little verandah, perched on a hillside and looking directly onto the dam-style water hole – have a certain charm. (Way too wet to attract wildlife at this time of year, but the water hole is probably great in the dry season.)

We ate in the camp's restaurant that night – it was buzzing with local and foreign guests. The food was standard, but the menu surprised us with its line-up – even Thai curry was on offer, but we decided that was better left to the experts …

We retired to the yowling of a jackal and in the night I awoke to catch the guttural grunting of a lion.

DAY 4
Main Camp via Zuurberg and Swaershoek passes to Mountain Zebra NP (238km)
Leg time without stops: 5 hours

Today was a gravel day – finally! We were going to climb into big skies to conquer a few passes.

EXIT MAIN CAMP (2KM); LEFT ONTO R342 FOR 1.5KM, THEN RIGHT ONTO R335 (GRAVEL) FOR 45KM

First, we skirted the border of Addo, with pine forests and citrus orchards to our left, driving north on a badly eroded road affected by washaways, to get into the northern Zuurberg Section of the park. Heavily wooded hills of bristly thorned acacias and tangled thicket were interspersed with lanky euphorbia forests, flowering cactuses and groves of succulent flat-leaved crassula with horizontal coral heads.

We climbed Doringnek Pass through impenetrable vegetation, with high banks encroaching onto an extremely narrow road. We stopped to marvel at the sheer drop of the valley, euphorbias pushing up for air as they thrust through the forest canopy below.⑫ Then we were running al-

---

Addo eco-activities
This is an enormous, sprawling park (1800km^2), divided into six sections and covering five of the country's nine biomes.

Darlington and Kabouga sections: Bedrogfontein 4x4 Trail: 45km / 6 hours, between Darlington and Kabouga sections (overnight at Kabouga Cottage, Mvubu Camp Site, Fisherman's Cottages or the luxury Darlington Lake Lodge in Darlington Section). Terrain: riverine thicket, Afromontane forest, fynbos, arid Nama Karoo. Optional Grade 5 river crossing, low range required. Canoeing on river.

Zuurberg Section: Guided mountain horse trails (overnight at Narina Tented Bush Camp). Hiking trails: Cycad Trail – 1 hour; Doringnek and natural river pool – 12.5km / 4–5 hours; overnight trail to Narina Tented Bush Camp near Witrivier – 10km / 1 day.

Addo Main Camp Section: Guided and self-drive game-viewing; guided horse trails; bird hide.

Colchester Section: Southern, wilder part of central game park area; self-drive game-viewing. Fishing, boating, canoeing, ferry trips – enquire at reception.

Woody Cape Section: Hiking trails: Tree Dassie Trail – 7km / 3–4 hours; Alexandria Hiking Trail – 36km / 2 days (overnight in Langebos huts in forest, Woody Cape Hut on coastline). Terrain: indigenous forest, pristine coastline, dune cliffs, coastal fynbos, coastal dune field.

most across the top of the mountain, now denuded of vegetation. At 593m we were surprised to encounter a row of charming Victorian-style cottages in soft pastel shades lining the mountain slope: Zuurberg Mountain Village, gateway to the Zuurberg Pass. Worth a try sometime, we decided, making a mental note.

In the Zuurberg Pass now, we continued hugging the mountainside on an increasingly narrow, waterlogged, muddy track, where only mountain cabbages retained a tenuous hold. It was rutted, stony and veined with rivulets, the road edge protected only by spaced slabs of stone. Little reassurance … it was a long and very bouncy tumble into the valley below. A rock face in the pass was painted with the words 'Woodfield's Krantz 1855'. They worked hard, those early pass-builders. Making slow progress at 10–15kph, we crested at 720m, now in montane fynbos territory, surrounded by leucadendrons and pretty white and purple ericas.

After descending through a mix of wooded slopes and grassland, it was time for a caffeine shot; a slew of wooden cabins belonging to Addo Elephant Backpackers (looking a little forlorn in winter) seemed the right place at which to stop.

It wasn't the end of the pass, though. After our break, we continued climbing to 882m on a similarly washed-away track, with puny stone slabs feigning a measure of protection against skidding off into the abyss. We had helicopter views over the mountain grasslands and Little Fish River valley.

After a descent through bitter aloes and leafy acacias, we passed Ann's Villa, a historical Victorian homestead with the tiny Blacksmith Museum attached. It was time to leave the Zuurberg Pass.

Our stomachs were rumbling to rival an elephant's …

✝ LEFT ONTO R335 (GRAVEL, TOWARDS SOMERSET EAST) FOR 11KM, RIGHT AT STONEFOUNTAIN (57KM)

We were now on a well-maintained gravel road, heading into the Karoo landscape: rolling hills dotted with round-headed shrubs and wiry trees, interspersed with agaves, sweet-thorns and coral-crowned crassula. More Karoo-like you can't get, with lone zinc-roofed homesteads, cranking windmills,⑮ ostriches and woolly goats and sheep, whose mass of tiny kids and lambs gambolled about. Rock Kestrels and lovely Pale Chanting Goshawks made us pause once in a while.

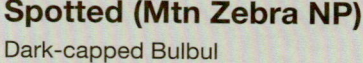

Spotted (Mtn Zebra NP)
Dark-capped Bulbul
African Red-eyed Bulbul
Acacia Pied Barbet
Chestnut-vented Tit-babbler
Ant-eating Chat
Malachite Kingfisher
Spoonbill
Verreaux's (Black) Eagle
Pale Chanting Goshawk⑬

✝ LEFT ONTO R63 FOR 3KM TO SOMERSET EAST

The large volumes of rain had taken a toll on the road, which was heavily potholed. Roller-flat grasslands, broken only by solitary aloes, were the perfect stage for elegant Secretary Birds. The trip, so far, had taken us five hours. Even though our stomachs were rumbling to rival an elephant's, Somerset East's lacklustre offerings compelled us to push on to Cradock, an hour away.

✝ LEFT ONTO R63 (CRADOCK) FOR 15KM; RIGHT ONTO GRAVEL R337 (VIA SWAERSHOEK PASS) FOR 77KM, THEN LEFT ONTO R337 TO CRADOCK FOR 2KM

Everything was much greener now. Thickly wooded hills were cluttered with aloes; instead of the denuded, white-spiked acacias of Addo, here they bristled greenly. From the river valley we climbed toward rocky mountaintops, peering down onto muddy waterways. The road looped along the edge of a series of interlocking hills as we passed farms with names like Doornbosch, Doornhoek and Groot Vlakte – an allusion to the intransigence of life in the Karoo.

Ahead of us, a sugarloaf mountain sprinkled with snow lived up to its image. Our mountain-framed vista opened up to a linked chain of flat rock tops, their snow-dusted ramparts resembling grey ash. We were now in the Swaershoek Pass, and the ash shroud was solidifying into ragged patches of snow. We'd hit 1600m(!), from where a vertiginous drop disappeared into the void, with a dead ringer for Table Mountain arcing to our left. Next was Maraiskloof, where dramatic cliffs rose vertically to either side, vacillating between rock wall and shattered-boulder slopes. The road, although graded, was stony, rutted and pockmarked with potholes.

Cradock had one redeeming feature: a Spar! Lunch was a dry cheese sandwich. It tasted like caviar.

☞ Left onto N10 (Graaff-Reinet) for 5km, left onto R61 for 6km, left into Mountain Zebra NP for 13km

After signing in at the gate, we drove 12km to the park's reception. Our roof for the night was a family cottage, one of a row set into thorny acacias and *taaibos*. Most appealing were the roof-height sliding doors of the kitchenette/lounge and the bedrooms, which opened onto the surrounding vegetation, and the patio braai area off the lounge. The main selling point? A huge fireplace. And that's where we settled in for the night, three kings in our armchairs drawn up to the flames.

DAY 5
Mountain Zebra NP
Juriesdam 4x4 Trail (Grade 2 with rocky ascents/descents; 9.5km)
Leg time without stops: 1 hour

Since we've already explored, and covered in considerable detail, Mountain Zebra NP in our first book, I won't dwell too much on it here. Our purpose in returning was to tackle the two newish 4x4 trails in the park.

What we did love this time was seeing the landscape in the finery of a changed season. Contrasting with the emerald and jade greens of our last rain-kissed Karoo trip, the palette now was wheat, russet, copper and gold, but no less beautiful. It was 3°C, the right temperature for the snow-dust fairy to be visiting these parts – the upper mountain slopes were heavily spotted and striated with frosting.

On our way to the Juriesdam Trail, the beauty of the mountains lured us up the Kranskop Loop, usually open to all vehicles, but this time with a warning sign across the road. We decided our vehicles would handle what was obviously a snow-bound section … and, yes, there were snow banks, and it was wet, muddy and stony, but nothing the Freelander and Toyota Hilux couldn't handle. On a level with the snow ridges, we came eyeball to eyeball with a Verreaux's (Black) Eagle riding the air currents, feathers splayed on giant wings. Its yellow beak and luminous white details on the rump were so clear, we felt utterly exhilarated. Next came a dark morph of either a Booted Eagle or a Steppe Buzzard – we couldn't quite discern which one it was. Then came a Pale Chanting Goshawk. We also ploughed through a terraced mass of water cascading over a slab of granite.

After a much-called-for coffee break (it's exhausting inhaling so much beauty) at the Weltevrede Picnic Spot on the Kranskop Loop, we girded our loins for the Juriesdam. The intention was to get to the top of a steep plateau – and then descend at the other end.

We'd hardly had time to breathe in deeply when we were faced with a sharply angled rise upward … the track littered with lodged rocks, loose boulders, mud holes, ruts and

dongas. At times we hovered in a state of suspension, poised between advancing and rolling backwards onto devouring boulders (hey, we never claimed to belong to the 'main manne' brigade), while my pounding heart was put through its paces. We bounced and swayed over shifting rocks, slipping and sliding through mushy tracks while trying not to catch our undercarriage on the elevated *middelmannetjie*, intermittently fording swift-running watercourses.

Then we had some respite as we trundled across the top of the plateau, marvelling at how red hartebeest and mountain zebra manage to pick their way to such elevations.

Too soon we were forced to tackle the descent, which seemed so much steeper than the trip up. At one point, the Freelander was almost vertical, nose down, tail in the air. It took all I had not to leap out and leave Hirsh to his own adrenaline rush. With the vehicle in Descent Control mode, we hesitated a fraction too long on the crest of a slope and the vehicle, its slow steady progress interrupted, went charging down the precipitous incline, wheels grinding loudly as Descent Control worked to gain stability at speed as we clambered over boulders and bounced into dongas.

It was adventure we went looking for, and it was adventure we got.

DAY 6
**Mountain Zebra NP, Nieu-Bethesda and Weltevreden Guest Farm (135km)
Leg time without stops: 2½ hours**

We awoke to a thick crust of ice on the windscreens; it was a chilled -3°C. We thought we'd left these kinds of temperatures behind in New York City!

Time to tackle the second 4x4 trail, the Sonnenrust Loop in the park's northern sector. The boys felt it necessary to let down their tyres to 1.8 bars, so they did.

**Sonnenrust 4x4 Trail (Grade 2, rocky ascents/descents; 14km)
Optional extra: Grade 4 Umngeni Trail – too Rambo for us!**

We set off from a small wood of gaunt trees with gnarled and twisted trunks. This opened out to a great expanse of wheaten grassland in which the weird thin arms of the leafless worm bush were conspicuous. The plains game (and vervet monkeys) were out and at play: kudu, springbok, black wildebeest – frisky and at full gallop, cream bushy tails thrashing. And, only at the highest elevations, mountain zebra … just living up to their name.⑯

At first the track was deceptively benign, although deeply rutted. Then we got into sharply rising inclines embedded with boulders, followed by sharp dips. The most challenging section was a series of rocky S-bends, where the boys had to swing the wheel left and right to avoid careening into the sweetthorns (not so sweet when they've skewered your ear lobe to your lip). Despite our rocking and swaying and bouncing, the Freelander was as sure-footed as a mountain goat. (Keith's Toyota Hilux Raider needs no comment.)

The views at the top were breathtaking: we were in a sea of yellow grasses ringed by snow-cloaked peaks straight out of Switzerland. On one horizon was a layered finger cake of ridges in russets and browns, on another a distant haze of mountains in blue, mauve and indigo.

Aside from the few steep rocky legs, the trail isn't technically difficult, but what it does do is give you open sesame to an undeveloped sector of the park you'd normally never have the chance to explore. An added bonus was that, during the entire morning, the only other vehicle we encountered (and that was at a distance) was a SANParks jeep.

Our greatest moment of excitement came when we followed an elusive moving shadow in the grasslands. At first we believed it to be a hyena, but eventually its brown-silver coat, side stripes and the dark ridge on its spine took on the shape of an aardwolf! First time ever we've seen one. Usually a nocturnal creature, in winter it apparently emerges later in the day to feed on termites.

19

🚏 To park exit for 14km), left onto R61 (Graaff-Reinet) for 80km

It went from springbokkies to *skapies* as we traversed flat grasslands and low-slung plateaus before starting to climb the Wapadsberg Pass. At 1750m we were in snow-patch and white-peak country. If we hadn't just recently survived -15°C snow blizzards in New York, we'd probably have been out of the car, making snowballs. But right now we were a teeny bit blasé.

It was back to big skies, with only cows and crows for company.

🚏 Right onto N9 (Middelburg); after 1km, left onto gravel for 27km to Nieu-Bethesda

You can't miss the sharp, pointy nose of Kompasberg (Compass Mountain) jutting skyward out of the flat plateau. Its snow-shrouded bulk reminded us of Zermatt.⑰

The eccentric town of Nieu-Bethesda was simply a lunch stop on the way to our farmhouse overnight accommodation, Weltevreden Guest Farm. But what a quirky *plek* to take a break! A tiny village of sand roads, no street lights and very little signage, other than a couple of vintage signposts that have managed to endure. Time, seriously, has stood still here. The rumpled collection of buildings, many with old, rusted tin advertisements fixed to the walls, exude a decided air of neglect, but you get the feeling this is carefully orchestrated and just the way the locals like it.⑱ Heaven forbid it becomes the new Darling! Besides the ever-intriguing Owl House (featured in *Our Top 4x4 Trips*), the spacious, light-filled Karoo Lamb Deli, with its laid-back air and its *stoep,* was the perfect place to hang out for a while.

Later, we discovered that the happening spot was, in fact, across the Gats River, at the Two Goats Brewery and Deli. While the boys sat in die garden and sampled the home-brewed beer (kegs ingeniously installed inside two old enamel

... oops, being a Sunday the gatekeeper was off duty

Frigidaires with a tap protruding from the side), I walked one of two giant labyrinths on the property. Fashioned from well-established but meticulously clipped rosemary bushes, one was a square, the other circular. Very peace-inducing; you'd be surprised at the quiet insights that creep up on you.

🚏 From Owl House, right onto Hudson St, left onto Martin St, to Weltevreden Farm for 13km

Cows and cactus fields accompanied us to Weltevreden, where our whitewashed Old Cape-style farmhouse (with modern amenities), overlooking a small dam, had big windows and a trellised vine to one side. There were pigs and sheep in the fields, and a friendly dog on our *stoep*. The house was lovingly furnished with some Old Cape-style pieces, our beds were warmed by electric blankets (nirvana) and reading matter included Athol Fugard's *The Road to Mecca* (which Keith read in bed in one sitting).

The beautiful late-afternoon light was too much to pass up on. A run was called for (while the *manne* set about doing braai-related things), which was lucky for the Dutch couple I encountered, whose mud-engulfed Nissan 2WD was deeply entrenched in a slushy, rutted water drift. Earlier, the same crossing had been a little treacherous for us, but that's what 4x4s are for. I reassured the helpless couple that we had all the right tow ropes and retraced my steps, knowing that Hirsh and Keith would be itching to test out their recovery gear. It wasn't even a challenge. The Hilux, using a rope, gently eased the Nissan out backwards and we waved two eternally grateful visitors back to firmer territory.

DAY 7
**Weltevreden Farm to Camdeboo NP and Noorspoort Farm (199km)
Leg time without stops: 4½ hours**

🚏 Right at Weltevreden farm entrance onto gravel for 34km

It was a gorgeous, clear day despite the light frost. The grassed kopjes were olive and khaki among the rock outcrops, conical hills and tabletop plateaus. The sense of infinite space

offer much respite. The temperature had cracked 40°C.

What makes this park attractive is its rocky hauteur – mainly sandstone structures, but in places you see unusual cracked and peeling layers, neat squares pulling away from the main rock like a thick lining. In the valley, where our camp stood, is a bulwark of red and cream cliffs, scoured by wind and rain. Around the K2 hill, heavily bouldered hill outcrops dominate the landscape.

We took the River Road drive, its tangled and thick vegetation permitting a sneak preview of a bull elephant and a few impala. At the river, the boundary fence – double layers of electrification – had been thoroughly trampled by elephant and clearly no efforts were being made to rectify this. And, to our great dismay, we could see cattle grazing on the flood plain of the Limpopo! Whatever happened to the threat of foot and mouth disease? (*See* an interesting web-link on the ongoing cattle issue under Web Resources.)

With a lovely orange glow gilding rocks and baobabs,③ we meandered through riverine bush, which, with its knobbly-trunked sycamore figs, resembled a goblin's forest. Beyond this, desiccated savannah plains were covered in scraggly sweet-thorn acacias; here we spotted Natal Francolin and Swainson's Spurfowl, the latter with a striking cherry-red eye patch and throat. Wildebeest, kudu and plenty of springbok also caught our attention.

... the switch of a tail curled like a perfect question mark on a rock face ... leopard!

As we headed home, the switch of a tail curled like a perfect question mark caught my eye on a rock face. There, in the gathering dusk, lodged between sandstone and a rock fig, was a leopard cracking its way through a kill it had dragged up to the crevice. We were floored. A great pity that the blanket of night was fast descending and the leopard was quickly dissolving into the shadows. But nothing could suppress our elation. We were on cloud nine.

Mapungubwe rocks
♦ The rock knolls and cliffs in this park are mainly sedimentary (sandstone and siltstone) or metamorphic (highly weathered gneisses), i.e. granite or conglomerate rock that has undergone high-temperature and/or intense-pressure changes.
♦ Just before Leokwe Main Camp, there's a fascinating rocky stretch of wavy flow lines and a softly moulded knobbly surface, as if the rock has bubbled up from water. My theory was that layered sedimentation was exposed to water action aeons ago. It seems not. Most likely it consists of layered, undulating bands of weathered gneiss.

Although all the elements were right for our bush-camp stay – full moon rising, beautiful A-frame wood and canvas units angled towards the cliffs, large kitchen deck and braai area cradled by a massive boulder – some bright spark had forgotten to flick on the power mains. There was no electricity to support the

batteries to the solar panels. This meant no fridges, no fans, no lights. It was 39°C. To add insult to injury, a tiny pool (with a bath plug) built into the rocks on a west-facing hill was bone-dry.

We were far too remote to consider returning to the main gate, and anyway, it was closed up by now. The mood was a tad black – particularly after we'd sweated up and down a long meandering path, lugging ammo boxes, bags and firewood.

We made the best of it. A suspiciously abundant supply of candles proved useless; the heat had rendered them pliable as fondant icing. Luckily we had the moonlight and a battery-operated lamp.

Later, from our balcony, we listened to the sounds of the night … a barn owl nearby, munching antelope below.

DAY 2
Vhembe Trails Camp to Leokwe Main Camp, excluding game-viewing loops (13km)

We awoke to blue wildebeest grazing in the valley and hornbills flitting between trees. At 07:00 it was already 26°C; by 08:00 it had leapt to 30°C.

Our vehicles headed out towards the Kanniedood 4x4 Loop in the extreme east of the park. The yellowed roots of rock figs snaked impossibly skyward, and beautiful, pendulous, creamy flowers hung from gigantic baobabs. A bull elephant, brusquely shoving aside dry, leafless trees to strip the bark from healthy trees and funnel it into his mouth, was the precursor for a stretch of desolate waste-

... staring at us through deep black-hole eyes, a Pel's Fishing Owl

land that was utterly stripped of its vegetation: skeletal trees had been knocked over, uprooted or dumped on their crowns – a sobering reminder of the destruction elephants can wreak on their environment.

The exciting part of this park is its truly wild terrain. Surrounded by brittle, papery mopane woodland, rocky hills and bouldered outcrops, we bounced over rock shelves, embedded boulders and stony tracks. There were intense corrugations and very steep ascents and descents. High clearance is a definite prerequisite here. The 4x4 track rose to the crest of a ridge with wonderful views into a deep narrow valley, after which a series of savannah-covered hills marched into the heat haze. The challenge was getting to the foot of the crest, via a near-vertical slope, but the Freelander's descent control handled it slowly and surely. Not so the beating of my heart. Keith's Toyota Hilux simply rumbled solidly down.

All the water points marked on our map were bone-dry (rain was somewhat late this year), but a pair of gemsbok, a steenbok, heaps of impala[11] and little squirrels in a tree knew how to survive in these dry conditions. Twice we saw a Martial Eagle planing above.

At reception, our lament over the lack of power at Vhembe Trails Camp was met with a shrug; no one seemed particularly concerned.

When we piled out at Leokwe, all our petty irritations instantly dissolved. After our wilderness camp, this was sheer luxury. The gathering of orange-brown rondavels, with attractive stepped-thatch roofs nestled into rock cliffs and high boulders, exuded class: slate and clay floors, lazily turning fans, air conditioning, thick quality folds of curtaining and embroidered bed linen. The kitchen/dining/living room was airy and spacious and the two bedrooms tastefully furnished. Artfully framed pictures of some of Mapungubwe's treasures, among them the iconic gold rhino, were hung throughout. Outside, a wooden deck, sheltered by a ceiling of stakes, overlooked what is probably a river during rains. And a nice touch was the outdoor shower, hidden behind a curve of wooden stakes. We even saw the butt end of an elephant ambling by in the distance.

A boon was the centrally located pool built into surrounding boulders – in the 40°C heat it was gently lukewarm. No matter, it was as good a place as any to congregate.

Treetop Walk
We'd signed up for a guided night drive and decided to try out this elevated walk before meeting up with our ranger. From the parking area, a beautifully constructed boardwalk⑤ curves through feathery ana trees with their apple-ring pods and passes some stately specimens of fever tree,⑩ their yellowed trunks lending a ghostly air to the woods. Benches have been built in strategic places and the end point of the walkway gives onto suspended views to Botswana across the broad, flat flood plain of the Limpopo. Further east, at the Confluence Viewpoints, a long, winding path leads to various sweeping vistas that focus on the spot where the Shashe River, dividing Botswana and Zimbabwe, meets the Limpopo.

A wild wind was blowing as we gazed onto the narrow flow of water meandering through the sand. Spotted and striped bushbuck grazed beneath us, while a herd of impala, two warthog and some baboons loitered at the river. That is, of course, if you ignore the cattle wandering all over the banks.

Guided night drive
The start of our night drive at the main gate was perfectly timed: we watched in awe as a pumpkin-orange moon heaved itself into the sky. Our driver and guide, Leonard, proved to be worth his full weight in salt. With the exception of elephant, his spotlight picked out most of the wildlife we'd seen in the day. Then things revved up a notch. He'd been aware of lion in the area earlier, but there only being seven of these cats in the entire park, we hardly dared to hope. Yet there they were: a heavy-maned male, a female and two cubs hiding in scrub against a rock slope, with their kill. How Leonard spotted them is beyond us, but in the glare of the spotlight the adults swiftly herded the young ones deeper into the vegetation. The male returned to conceal himself (or so he believed) behind overhanging brush; the female eventually prowled back to continue with her meal. We could hear the cracking of the bones from our seats in the Jeep.

So elated we thought it couldn't get better, we were passing a tiny waterhole at Zebra Pan when Leonard screeched to a halt. Here, staring at us through deep black-hole eyes, sat an enormous brown Pel's Fishing Owl. It flew to a nearby branch, perfectly poised towards us, and gazed unblinking in our direction for a protracted length of time. Now, we know enough about bird-watching to understand that this is a really rare sighting …

The next surprise was a spotted hyena, a nocturnal animal we don't get to see too often. And then we saw a Black Stork, comically standing poker-straight in a tree.

Spotted
Martial Eagle
Wahlberg's Eagle
African Hawk-Eagle
African Grey Hornbill
Red-billed Hornbill ⑥
Cinnamon-breasted Bunting
White-fronted Bee-eater
Lilac-breasted Roller ②
Purple Roller
White-crested Helmet Shrike
Meves's Starling
Cape Glossy Starling
African Pied Wagtail
Red-billed Buffalo-Weaver
Pied Kingfisher
Yellow-billed Stork
Goliath Heron
Grey Heron
Black-winged Stilt
(400 bird species in the park)

⑥

Exhilarated, we returned to Leokwe to sit on the deck, toast our success with a glass of wine and relive our experience. There, we were visited by an interminably curious small-spotted genet, hoping for some nourishment but scurrying away the minute it felt threatened.

DAY 3
Leokwe Main Camp to Limpopo Forest Tented Camp, excluding game-viewing loops (27km)

At 07:30, to the distinctive fast-descending murmur of the Emerald-spotted Wood Dove, we made an

early start from the main gate towards the great hill of Mapungubwe. We'd booked a guided excursion (mandatory) with a coolly dreadlocked heritage tour guide, Cedric Sethlako. ⑦

Mapungubwe Cultural Tour

The heat was already suffocating but thankfully Cedric's in-depth knowledge and wicked sense of humour distracted us. On being asked whether he'd ever had to use the rifle he was carrying, he replied thoughtfully, 'Those who know me leave me well alone.'

After looking at a reconstructed timeline at an excavated transection of archaeological digs (including domestic animal bones) carried out at the base of Mapungubwe, we set about tackling the 147 sandstone stairs hewn into the side of the oval-shaped rock bastion – 300m in length and 30m high.

What we saw on the crest were subtle yet fascinating signs of what was once a king's settlement – archaeologists have excavated three royal graves here. It's believed the hilltop was inhabited for about 70 years, from 1220–1290CE. Radiocarbon dating, artefacts and charred remains of millet, sorghum and beans point to a once wealthy, technologically advanced society; they were metalworkers, subsistence farmers and herders who bartered with Swahili traders, and also had contact with monsoon traders from the East.

The royal burial ground is an exposed rock shelf that was once covered in 1.5m of soil. It was here all the gold artefacts were unearthed (see Quick Summary panel) together with the bodies. We got to see grinding stones, small holes in the rock where poles were inserted for shelter, a large circular indentation which could have been the foundation for a hearth (signs of clay, dung and gravel remain), and a huge oval water storage area and many smaller ones. There are also a couple of good examples of a *morabaraba,* or *mankala,* board, a game in which small stones are placed in circular indentations in a rock slab.

Cedric took us to the edge of the rock kingdom – which, besides the lovely breeze, had impressive 360° views onto the surrounding rock kopjes, sandy flood plain and Shashe River – where he solemnly told us about the 'proposal rock'.

Mapungubwe Hill: a quick summary

- Mapungubwe Hill is part of a historical triangle: Mapungubwe, Great Zimbabwe and the Mmamagwa Ruins in Mashatu, Botswana, once settled by the Iron Age Zhizo people. The Mapungubwe society is believed to have developed out of the Zhizo culture.
- The mountain refuge is the first tangible proof of class hierarchy: the king physically removed himself from his common subjects, with only his royal aides living beside him on the hill. The common people were settled around the foot of Mapungubwe.
- Archaeological excavations here revealed evidence of successive stages of human cultural development, from Stone Age nomadic hunter-gatherers to Bronze Age Swahili traders, Late Iron Age forerunners of the Bantu-speaking people and, finally, agriculturalists and cattle herders.
- Gold artefacts found in and around the royal graves include the famous gold-foil rhinoceros and sceptre and bowl; gold bangles, anklets and beads; ivory armbands; glass and copper beads, and discs of ostrich eggshell. (At the time of writing, all artefacts were on display at the University of Pretoria. The intention is to move these to the national park's architecturally impressive Mapungubwe Interpretive Centre, officially open as of the end of 2012.)
- It's believed that at the end of the 13th century, an increasing population outgrew its resources: agricultural land, grazing and water. This would have led to a decrease in barter commodities, persuading the monsoon traders to focus on Great Zimbabwe instead.
- A fossil of a sleeping dinosaur can be viewed nearby and ancient dinosaur footprints can be viewed at Pontdrift, on the Limpopo River.

Here, at the precipice, suitors would line up their beloved ones and demand that they decide between marriage … and certain death (apparently there were bones below to prove the untimely demise of some unlucky [maybe strong-willed?] women). Deadpan, he ended with: 'Then they'd have to drink Red Bull, because it gives you wings.' Only now did he crack up and admit that the entire story was a fabrication.

Tshugulu Eco Trail (35km; 4½ hours)
Despite the 43°C heat wave at 12:30, it was time to test out the eco trail (at least we could slink into the chilled cocoon of air conditioning). It started in very open, stunted mopane woodland: red sand, emerald new growth and the tiny-leaf-encrusted branches of *Boscia foetida* – smelly shepherd's tree – all of which densely encroached on the road. At intervals, tiny 'golden rhino' icons guided the way.

Signs of elephant destruction were almost immediate – the earth was littered with branches, tree trunks and discarded roots, often requiring us to take tight turns around them. The mopane gave on to thorn scrub and lots of *Commiphora* trees on intense brick-red soils, with massive baobabs getting in a look-see. Of stately giraffe there were plenty (although skittish) lingering beneath the baobabs or hotfooting it with their stiff-necked gait. A tiny baby with furry little knobs had seemingly been left to fend for itself. Bulky eland, a huge herd of wildebeest and even very scarce waterbuck were around. We spied an African Hawk-Eagle and had a great sighting of an African Harrier Hawk (Gymnogene) with its funny flattened head and garish eye mask.

We were now travelling alongside the deep channel of a dry riverbed; we were surrounded by rugged rock outcrops, tall kopjes⑧ and colossal boulders shedding an outer skin. What followed can only be described as serious bundu-bashing, with some veering off-course and retracing of steps thrown in. S-bend turns were so tight, reversing was necessary; paths were blocked by snapped trees; tracks were barely there; twisting, dipping, up, down … But nowhere was there a sign of the hordes of elephant reputedly ruling these parts. Not one.

At the top of a ridge, we had magnificent views onto a valley with a great rock monolith and acid-green mopanes, a series of ascents and descents clearly visible. No pachyderms. As we stepped out of the vehicles, the 46°C hit us like a fiery breath. Walking to the edge of the escarpment was like ploughing through a blast furnace. A tall Kori Bustard agreed, beak hinged open as it took slow, prim steps.

Then it was silver cluster-leafs and candelabra trees and boulders cleaved by rock figs as we bounced through an otherworldly stone landscape and across rock shelves. A little do-it-yourself was involved: shifting wood, stamping down branches, restraining twigs.

Then we found a steaming heap of dung. And there was the elephant, right beside the track. Excitement all round.

Next was a small family – male, female, two babies and an older sibling, their trunks like snorkels as they cooled themselves and curled them

> *… serious bundu bashing, S-bend turns, some veering off-course and retracing of steps …*

77

deftly around tender mopane leaves to stuff them into their mouths. Then it was open season: another group of seven, some giraffe, and finally, at a wind-pumped water hole, a large elephant herd with a teeny muddied baby.⑨ For an instant we thought we might be charged at as a female started moving towards us, ears flapping furiously. It wasn't clear whether she was warning us or was simply bothered by the heat, but she didn't carry it through. Lucky for us. We were very pleased with ourselves. At least we could report that elephant still reigned along the Tshugulu Eco Trail. It was 17:00 and the temperature was still 44°C; it had taken us a full 4½ hours to complete the trail, but in terms of terrain, scenery and wildlife, we'd loved every minute.

Limpopo Forest Tented Camp
Termed wood and canvas 'tents', these units are so much more: the kitchen area and bathroom are built with solid walls; the bedrooms, roof and windows are canvas; and the floor, shelves, cupboards and furniture are in solid wood. A little suffocating and hot in 40°C temperatures, but what do

Identify your bushveld trees

Wild raisin (*Grewia flava*) – twiggy bush, tiny leaves curled inward, small red-brown berries (December to April)
Knob-thorn (*Acacia nigrescens*) – trunk covered in knobby thorns, leaf stems carry little paired leaflets, crown looks very much like maidenhair fern
Lowveld cluster-leaf (*Terminalia prunioides*), a *Combretum* (bushwillow) species – untidy, long trailing branches, tiny leaves clustered at ends of branches, fruit is a flat, winged seed, changing from red to purple to brown
White seringa (*Kirkia acuminata*) – mass of leaflets along leaf stems, leaflets crowded at ends of branches, crown looks lacy from a distance, often on rocky outcrops
Mountain seringa (*Kirkia wilmsii*) – similar to above but leaflets tinier, appearing more crowded at ends of branches, very lacy/feathery, often has brown clusters of seed pods
Nyala (*Xanthocercis zambesiaca*) – colossal trees with an enormous crown, stout trunk grooved and dented in older trees, very glossy green leaves
Large fever berry (*Croton megalobotrys*) – always along flat watercourses, big leaves with serrated edges ending in a point, green to yellowish-brown berries

Commiphora species
Hairy corkwood/*kanniedood* (*C. africana*) – smooth, grey, ringed bark, peels in papery scrolls, thin thorny branches, little three-leaved clusters
Zebra-bark corkwood (*C. merkeri*) – grey bark with dark, warty horizontal dashes (the zebra stripes), peels in yellowish strips
White-stem corkwood/*kanniedood* (*C. tenuipetiolata*) – similar to previous, has grey-yellow papery bark
Velvet corkwood (*C. mollis*) – long, trailing branches, greenish to silvery-grey bark, flakes in thick discs

Spotted
- Heuglin's Robin
- Groundscraper Thrush
- Wattled Starling
- Dark-capped (Black-eyed) Bulbul
- Red-billed Buffalo-Weaver
- Meyer's Parrot

you expect? The tents crouch beside riverine forest (no sign of the Limpopo) under heaving nyala trees, scented-thorn acacias and apple-leaf trees. And … time to ululate … the camp has a decent-sized fenced pool.

After a much-needed swim, our last excursion of the day was a drive to the nearby Maloutswa Hide and water hole. We certainly got more than we bargained for. It was playtime at the zoo. As we crept in, an elephant was rubbing its earth-soiled body just metres from the hide opening while the rest of the troop was preparing to leave after a sticky session in thick, sucking mud.

Group after group trooped swiftly down, swished around in the mud bath, then turned tail and silently melted into the trees. Our main entertainment came from the tiniest baby pitter-pattering behind its mother, and its perplexity at its little straw of a trunk falling way short of the water. With haste it backed up and hared around the water hole to its older siblings, where it slipped and slid into a mud hole that all but swallowed it. We eventually located it, hanging with both front legs over a little ridge trying to scramble out.

The elephant herds were followed by a squabbling, shrieking squad of baboons, a shy and diffident steenbok and two twitchy black-backed jackal.

More successful a day we couldn't have asked for.

DAY 4
Limpopo Forest Tented Camp to Izintaba Private Game Reserve (367km)
Leg time without stops: 4½ hours

Since we were now in the extreme north of the country (and we had to start making our way back home again), it was crazy to pass up on the opportunity to visit a couple of South Africa's remoter national parks, Marakele being one. In the Limpopo province, Marakele is in the heart of the Waterberg – but distance demanded an intermediary stop, so it was to Izintaba Private Game Reserve we were headed.

> *It was playtime at the zoo …*

⨎ OUT OF PARK, RIGHT FOR 7KM, LEFT ON R572 TO ALLDAYS (56KM). EXIT WEST ON R572 (185KM)

The boys filled their vehicles in Alldays. We left on a very patchy tar and heavily potholed road, driving through thick green acacia thornveld and *Combretum* (bushwillow) woodland.

⨎ LEFT ON R510 TO LEPHALALE (ELLISRAS) FOR 38KM

Here, apparently, we officially entered the Waterberg area. A Pick n Pay in Lephalale was a convenient stop for restocking on supplies, and I finally identified my first marula tree – they were everywhere.

⨎ SOUTH OUT OF LEPHALALE ON R33 (VAALWATER) FOR 54KM

Thanks to the verdant, hilly country and the higher altitudes (we peered onto the treetops of densely wooded valleys), the temperature had dropped to a more palatable 36°. We chortled at a roadside series of building-high signs for a meat factory advertising, in giant yellow letters, boerewors, steak and even *ouma se gemmerbier*; then, when you'd passed the last one, a final sign with an arrow shouted 'Go Back, Biltong! Subtle.

⨎ LEFT ONTO GRAVEL AT VISGAT SIGN FOR 11KM; LEFT AT DOORNLAAGTE, AFTER 5KM, KEEP RIGHT FOR 10KM TO IZINTABA

Back in savannah country, we made a right turn and then proceeded left into Izintaba.

DAY 5
Izintaba Private Game Reserve

We loved Izintaba. Our thatched Bushbuck Cottage, decorated in bush lodge style (lanterns, baskets and grasses, clay pots, San-motif drapes), was airy and spacious. It had polished dung floors, large wooden windows and double doors opening onto a big treed garden with a thatched seating area and braai. A nearby pool, painted aquamarine-blue, was built into massive boulders⑫ and harboured a resident frog and some brightly accented lizards. We kept them company often.

The reserve has a 4x4 route which, although not technically difficult, serves up plenty of soft sand, rock

79

shelves and stony, uneven, rock-embedded sections,⑬ requiring slow and careful navigating. The bushveld here is lovely: shale-like terraces, brick-red conglomerate rock, grassland and dense woodland (look out for the peeling plane's scarlet-winged green berries and the big papery winged pods of the large-fruited bushwillow). And you can't miss the wild (red) syringa, a slender, many-branched tree with a flat spreading crown that exudes African bushveld.

Two separate Sunset Rock lookouts have decks on, or among, sandstone boulders, and the views over the tree canopy stretch to every horizon (lovely at the end of the day, too). The wildlife (although particularly skittish) isn't bad, either.

We saw enormous specimens of eland, waterbuck, blue wildebeest and Burchell's zebra, and startled a Black-chested Snake Eagle with beautiful white and black-barred underwings.

We agreed that this had been an ideal stopover for us, but equally good any time for an extended weekend of bush R&R. It comes highly recommended.

DAY 6

Izintaba Private Game Reserve to Marakele NP via Waterberg Meander (171km)
Leg time: 3½ hours

🛪 LEFT OUT OF IZINTABA TO SUKSES (18KM), RIGHT ONTO D972 (8KM), LEFT FOR 9KM, KEEP LEFT FOR 4KM, THEN RIGHT ONTO GRAVEL AT T-JUNCTION TO WATERBERG MEANDER (FOLLOW THE SIGNS) AND BOEKENHOUTSKLOOF (54KM)

A corrugated gravel road, lined to either side by game farms, eventually became rocky and stony, as we rose to beautiful high views over the heavily wooded Waterberg hills. That the permeable sandstone retains water is obvious, and countless underground springs feed a verdant swathe of deciduous forest.⑭ Following the 'yellow elephant' signs, we passed through woodland that was either open and grassed or close and thick, with patches of grassy savannah in-between. Most conspicuous among the acacias were colossal buttressed figs, but the day was quintessential bushveld: red road, green canopy, thick white clouds, cobalt sky. There are various meandering passes and viewpoints with expansive vistas onto treed river valleys and up to high rock kopjes (on Geelhoutkop I couldn't spy a single yellowwood among the acacias). Marakele NP, visible on the horizon, climbs to 2088m at

> **Spotted**
> Karoo Thrush
> Olive Thrush
> Red-headed Weaver
> Fiscal Flycatcher
> White-bellied Sunbird
> Greater Double-collared Sunbird
> Greater Blue-eared Starling
> Dark-capped Bulbul
> European Bee-eater
> Red-billed Oxpecker
> Black-chested Snake Eagle

its highest point and claims the loftiest spot in the Waterberg.

Soon we were deep in the belly of the mountains, rock-embedded slopes dwarfing us to either side, then rugged cracked sandstone cliffs taking their place. At some point our road was signposted Tarentaalstraat (Guineafowl Street), yet it was the sing-song 'piet-my-vrou' of the Red-chested Cuckoo that tailed us everywhere we tarried.

At Boekenhoutskloof turn left for 29km, right via Bakkers Pass to Marakele NP (49km)

Next, the high slopes fell away and we were in an enormous, flat, farmed valley lined by Waterberg hills in all shades of green (one row of connected buttresses carries the name Seven Sisters). Here, we had to be wary of domestic livestock on the road. Before long, we left the foot of the escarpment behind as we skirted the edge of the massif, rising rapidly towards Bakkers Pass. We paused for a Purple Heron in a dam and – to our utter bemusement – a herd of what appeared to be albino blesbok on a game reserve called Dinaka. These 'white blesbok' are *not* albino, but are the result of a mutation in colour that lends them an all-over grey-white hue. Very strange to behold.

The sandstone outcrops, marked with horizontal ridges, were now a rich russet-red, as were the earth embankments – all softened by lushly green foliage.

By the time we entered Marakele's park gates, we were in the valley again. Once more, no bird or tree lists were available at reception, but a mammal list was. Grinding and gnashing of teeth.

Lenong Viewing Point – nesting Cape Vultures

Anxious to make the most of the day, we decided to drive straight to the park's highest point (beneath a communications tower) to catch a glimpse of Marakele's breeding Cape Vultures – 800 pairs according to the SANParks website. Marakele National Park has a demarcated antelope sector and, beyond a gated 'subway', a predator sector (lion, leopard, brown hyena).

> ... the day was quintessential bushveld: red road, green canopy, thick white clouds, cobalt sky ...

Elephant and both species of rhino do a good job of hiding in the incredibly dense vegetation.

We'd hardly set out through antelope terrain when there were six or so vultures, gliding low over a hilltop. Luckily we got a good peek through our binoculars, as the Lenong Viewing Point was much harder work. Once through the subway and onto the Lenong Drive, the road climbed very quickly through densely packed vegetation towards a spectacular exposed-rock bastion⑮ which, up close, resembled shale in dramatic pancake layers. The road drop-offs were so sheer my stomach got that plummeting feeling, but the views onto the interleaved mountain massifs beneath us were equal to those of the two Verreaux's (Black) Eagles wheeling close by.

Beneath the cellphone tower, the views simply carried on to tomorrow, marred somewhat by a smoke haze from ... you guessed it, controlled burning. For a while, there was no sign of a single vulture. But as our eyes adjusted, slowly, slowly, we could make out between 15 and 20 dark silhouettes circling over the cliffs. The sun was sinking behind them so it wasn't going to get any better. But sightings of an African Harrier Hawk and Wahlberg's Eagle appeased us.

A short 4x4 route got the blood flowing through our veins again: a narrow, rutted, stony road twisted and turned through tightly-knit foliage; we crawled up and down angled inclines and declines and drank in more of the same beauty we'd experienced at the top. Unfortunately all the animal life was playing hide and seek in the tangled thicket; our only joy was a lonely hartebeest, some wildebeest, zebra, a few warthog, a klipspringer and a duiker.

Tlopi Tented Camp
Lining the Tlopi Dam, these wood and canvas 'tents' are relatively simple but somehow charming (zinc washbasins, metal lampshades with laser-cut designs, *great* shower), and their location is superb. Each has a big cantilevered deck at the edge of the water with a stone braai place. An attached kitchen unit has a floor-to-ceiling sliding glass door – and very well secured fridges, because … **watch out for the monkeys!** These ones are particularly brazen and highly mischievous, as some of our neighbours discovered when they had their food and belongings strung out between vehicle and tent.

A gentle breeze, our view onto the Waterberg hills, and the rose-tinted dam in the disappearing sun serenaded us gently into the evening.

DAY 7
Tlopi Tented Camp to main gates

Hirsh and I awoke to find Keith warring with vervet monkeys. They were poised fearlessly on the tent roof, the top beam of the kitchen's sliding door and various posts on the deck.

… watch out for the monkeys!

'C'mon, Keith Blackbeard Titley,' Hirsh egged him on. 'Go arrrrrr and repel the enemy!'

It indeed took much vigilance to move between kitchen and vehicle while we were packing up. The vervets were highly skilled at spotting a gap and whipping in and out before you had time to spin your head.

Spotted
Pin-tailed Whydah
Tawny-flanked Prinia
White-browed Scrub Robin
Mocking Cliff-Chat (male)
Diderick Cuckoo
Pied Kingfisher
Cattle Egret
Bronze-winged Courser

The drive between Tlopi and the main entrance gave us the opportunity to do some last-minute game-viewing and this time we were rewarded. A mother and baby elephant, not 5m in but deeply obscured by the leafy vegetation; three giraffe, one chewing with such vigour Hirsh quipped, 'He's found someone's Wrigleys'; a red hartebeest; and, *finally*, a female and baby white rhino clearly visible in open savannah grassland. Lesson learned: don't pooh-pooh the antelope sector!

And then we were at the main gate, and time for most people, sadly, to head home. Here many will try to get back to the N1 via either the R33 or R510. Because we still had such a long way to travel – all the way to the Western Cape – we stopped for another two nights: at Mokala National Park (Northern Cape) and Lemoenfontein Lodge, just outside Beaufort West. *See* panel for details.

Marakele and Mokala: a quick summary

♦ *Marakele* means 'place of sanctuary' in Tswana, referring to its protection of four of the Big Five (no buffalo).
♦ Marakele NP is best known for the nine elephants that were reintroduced from the drought-ravaged Tuli Reserve, where an individual had bought 30 elephants for resale to safari reserves and zoos. An outcry at the inhumane way the elephants were being treated led to an intervention by the WWF-SA, which donated the first nine pachyderms to Marakele.
♦ *Mokala* is the Setswana name for the camel-thorn acacia, which is prolific in the Northern Cape. It's the nesting ground of Sociable Weavers, and indigenous people use its gum, bark and seeds. Mokala is the country's newest park, opened in mid-2007.

Mokala NP (Kimberley)

What made Mokala a refreshing change from Marakele was its open terrain for wildlife visibility – grassland, Kalahari thornveld with prominent acacias (sweet-thorn, black-thorn, camel-thorn, umbrella-thorn), and rock outcrops. We stayed at the **Lilydale Rest Camp** in brick-and-thatched units on raised wooden decks, with stunning 180° views onto the Riet River in the valley below.⑰ **Mosu** is a sprawling thatched lodge on green lawns with different-sized units overlooking the veld and a pumped water hole (units number 2 and 3 have front-row seats).

During our overnight stay at Lilydale, besides the regular wildlife species, we were exhilarated to see three roan antelope and some russet, curly-horned tsessebe. But our absolute highlight was an enormous herd of buffalo stampeding to a water hole, which, with much territorial snorting and shoving (and urinating), they churned into a gloopy mud marsh. We drove through another herd, so close to the road we could stroke their heavy bosses. We chose not to.
Contact: www.sanparks.org/parks/mokala

Lemoenfontein Game Lodge (Beaufort West)

This old, airy, high-ceilinged hunting lodge (1850s), with its green zinc roof and wooden shutters, sits at the foot of a group of Karoo kopjes. Its spacious verandah, where meals are enjoyed, has expansive views over the Beaufort West Dam and Karoo plains. The bedrooms are luxurious – glass shower, white fluffy towels and mountains of pillows. As you drive up, expect to be greeted ('Helloooo!') by the resident blue and yellow parrot.
Contact: www.lemoenfontein.co.za

PLAN YOUR TRIP!

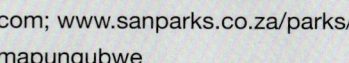

♦ **Web resources:**
Mapungubwe NP: www.mapungubwe.com; www.sanparks.co.za/parks/mapungubwe
Info on cattle roaming in Mapungubwe: www.sanparks.co.za/docs/parks_mapungubwe/roaming-cattle.pdf
Izintaba Lodge: www.izintabalodge.co.za
Marakele NP: www.sanparks.org/parks/marakele
Mokala NP: www.sanparks.org/parks/mokala
Lemoenfontein: www.lemoenfontein.co.za
♦ Extra tourist resources and contacts: *see* pages 158–160

OUR EXPERIENCE

♦ **Best move on the trip:**
We loved using newer, lesser-known parks as stepping stones (or incorporating them as part of the journey); it makes for a great adventure.

♦ **Worst move:**
Even though it was only just the beginning of summer, 46°C was a little high for us on the Richter scale of ambient air.

♦ **Our advice to you:**
We suggest you tackle this part of the country a month or so earlier than we did.

Eastern Cape – 11 mountain passes in 3 days

Round trip 624km starting/ending Lady Grey

What's so special about this route?

♦ We were dumbfounded at how exquisitely beautiful the Eastern Cape mountains, an extension of the Drakensberg, really are – who knew that this was right on our doorstep? Wake up, South Africa!

♦ These mountains are so much wilder, more remote, and less developed than those in KwaZulu-Natal (sorry, KZN!)

♦ A handful of the passes offer some pretty challenging 4x4 rough-riding – and they *always* come with a view

Trip summary

Features: Awesome passes, fearsome precipices, testing 4x4 driving
Trip duration: 3 days (624km)
Time of year: March (autumn)
Round trip: Starting and ending in Lady Grey
Road conditions: On the passes: stony, rocky (bouldered sections), rutted, bumpy, washaways. Tiffindell: *very steep* leg littered with boulders/concrete fragments, plus tight switchbacks.

Getting there

From Johannesburg: N1 to Bloemfontein, N6 to Aliwal North, R58 to Lady Grey
From Durban: (trip starting point: Maclear) N2 via Port Shepstone and Kokstad to R396 junction, R396 to Maclear
From Port Elizabeth: N2 to East London, N6 to Aliwal North, R58 to Lady Grey
From Cape Town: N1 to Gariep Dam, R58 via Burgersdorp to Aliwal North, R58 to Lady Grey

MORE INFORMATION: **Plan Your Trip Info: page 95**
Tourist Resources: pages 158–160
MAPS: **This Route's Map: pages 86–87**
Also in Road Atlas Section: pages 150–156

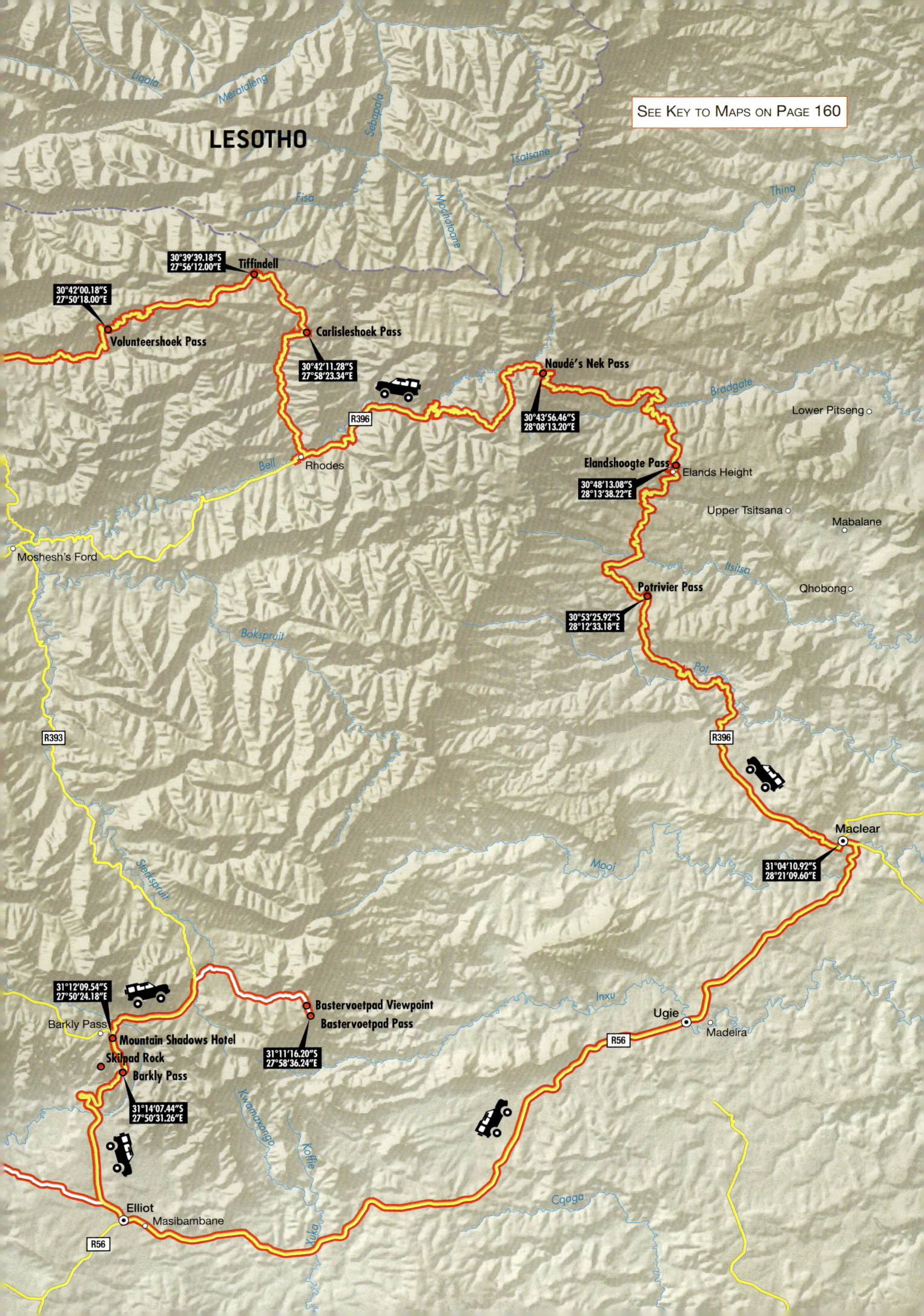

Lady Grey – overnight stop

🚩 Exit R58 into Lady Grey, right into Botha Street, left into George Street, follow signs to Comfrey Cottage

Our starting point in Lady Grey, a tiny village set amidst the sprawling, knobbly Witteberge foothills, was Comfrey Cottage guesthouse. ② Its little cottages, simply but nicely furnished (crisp white linen, ceiling fans, spacious modern bathroom), are crowded in by fruit trees. Peaches, plums, pears, pomegranates, quinces … and it's here that Gerda and George's alpacas, comical creatures in black, brown or cream with long necks, woolly knotted knees and furry caps, come to graze at night. The Witteberge, broken and ridged and green, are the lower hills of the great Drakensberg escarpment – and the perfect place to start exploring any number of impressive portals hacked through the sandstone mountains. This, of course, was the point of our trip.

After a breakfast of oatmeal porridge with a dash of whisky, and crumpets with home-made lemon curd and clotted cream, our vehicles rumbled heavily out of the gate.

DAY 1
PASSES – JOUBERTS', KRAAI RIVER, OTTO DU PLESSIS, BARKLY

Lady Grey to Mountain Shadows Inn near Barkly East (227km)
Allow a full day for this leg
Jouberts' Pass to Kraai River Pass: 3½ hours

🚩 From George St left into Cloete St, left into Walton St, after 1km turn left onto gravel track to Lady Grey Dam wall

A short and sharp 4x4 track takes you through blue gums to a place of broken cliffs and massive rock outcrops. 'Kloppers Draai 1922' is carved into a rock chunk and little braai places nestle into the boulders. But prettier even than the overhanging sandstone ledges and black-orange-caramel streaks is the streaming curtain of water dancing over the lip of the dam into a weir 25m below. You stand at the foot of it but can climb up to a viewpoint looking over Lady Grey. However, we felt too sad about the broken beer bottles and discarded tins that soiled an otherwise magical spot.

🚩 Return to gravel road, turn left for 1km, right to Witfontein viewsite (3km)

Heading first towards Witfontein Dam, a 6km 4x4 detour (high clearance required) took us to a set of communications masts for more views. It was hilly, rocky country, with fuzzy green, fat-fingered foothills and exposed cliffs. We climbed and climbed till we were in tufted montane grassland,

88

but stopped short of the masts because of heavy mud. This gave us views of Lady Grey and then the flat valley beyond.

⚑ Back to pass road, turn right, continue to R58 (45km)

This gravel pass road, traversing the Witteberge, is steep and winding, first skirting the mountain edge, then losing itself in the midst of the hills. A stone tablet at the crest commemorates five pass-building Jouberts. This is not rental-Uno country! The road surface is stony, rocky, rutted and bumpy. Look out for basalt outcrops along the western mountain spine – and prolific *ouhout* ('old wood'), a beautiful twisted, many-branched tree with rough, flaky bark and little serrated leaves.

Note the series of old information signs in an elegant blue cursive script – left by early pass builders, I wondered? There was no wind at Windpunt, but at Die Nek, the pass summit, a sign marked Hemel-op-Aarde ('heaven on earth') was more accurate. We were 408m above Lady Grey, and 2228m above sea level, and the vista into a verdant pastoral valley ringed by mountains was lovely.

Later, a short, steep descent had Hirsh chirping to Keith over the radio, 'Don't get a huge fright when you get to this drift.' It was called Skrikdrif.

The countryside flattened out. Our vehicles trundled past rolling green farmland, horse paddocks and fat cattle grazing with red-beaked White Storks! The quirky names of the many water drifts we crossed kept us amused: Car Sump Drift, Bridge over Ice Water, Kar Wegspoel Drif ('car washaway drift'). When we got to a drift with no name Hirsh quipped, 'Once you've had a *skrik*, lost a sump and been washed away, there's not much left to say …'

⚑ Left onto R58 (direction Barkly East)

At this point, the drive had taken us 3½ hours (over 56km). A hacked-rock portal called Grootnek Pass led us back into a green valley bowl surrounded by flat-topped ridges.

⚑ After 36km, turn left (direction New England)

Kraai River Pass (1 hour)

This 8km (one-way) detour off the R58 is not so much about the pass as it is about the rail reverses of a defunct single-gauge railway line, designed to get the train up and around the mountain.

You first cross the line (a non-event) in the valley. Pretty soon the dressed-stone Loch Bridge (December 1893) – a heritage site ③ – carries you over a pebble-strewn river with views to an elevated railway bridge supported by sturdy columns. The road

> *It was hilly, rocky country of fuzzy green, fat-fingered foothills …*

climbs above the river till, at the top of the pass where the road makes a sharp right, you see on the opposite mountain slope the long horizontal zigzags of the old railway line. There is room for two vehicles to pull over on the left-hand side, but if you drive a little further along, you peer directly onto the switchbacks.

In days of yore, steam locomotives were unable to tackle steep gradients (here, 1:36) and the mountain slopes were too curved for the steel line, so the long zigzags allowed the train to manoeuvre forward, then reverse along a section of line, puff forward along the next stretch, reverse again … and so on, till it got to the top of the pass! Ingenious. Rumour has it this is one of only two or three railway reverses in the world.

The parking verge is a perfect spot to pull over for coffee or lunch, where you gaze down onto the pretty red railway bridge and weeping-willow-fringed river.

Spotted

Speckled Mousebird
Pin-tailed Whydah
Yellow-rumped Widowbird
Drakensberg Siskin
Orange-breasted Rock-jumper
Common Stonechat
Mountain Chat
African Pied Starling
Greater Kestrel
Eastern Red-footed Falcon
Steppe Buzzard
Jackal Buzzard
Verreaux's (Black) Eagle

One of the original Class 19D steam locomotives gleams in a little park in Barkly East (opposite the sandstone church), all shiny black with red trim and white-rimmed wheels.

Otto du Plessis Pass (2½ hours)
The road rises from a river crossing and starts cutting into the side of a mountain as it steadily climbs. The magic of this pass is revealed only at the crest (2110m), like some open sesame at the escarpment of the Tsomo valley. After passing a cairn commemorating the opening of the pass, you encounter a massive drop-off that plunges to a faraway valley, offering views to forever. Heavy cloud hanging in the sky was casting lovely dappled shadows on the chartreuse mountain slopes,① like the webbed toes of a giant prehistoric creature. As we started descending, the earth fell away to either side of us and it was as if we were gliding suspended over the land. Domed hills, with exposed rock ridges lined in green fuzz, resembled octopuses; there were waterfalls, giant looming slopes and tight snaking bends. It was all quite exquisite and I wanted it never to end. But all too soon we were winding around the base of the mountain on a stony, muddy, washaway road.

After a little half-hour recovery exercise (*see* panel below) we continued, slipping and sliding in and out of dongas, through water, and over stones and embedded rock. We almost got stuck a second time, spinning sideways through a marsh and sending red mud spattering through our open windows. We had to laugh at a 40kph speed restriction sign; we were managing somewhere between 10 and 25kph. By the time we hit our gravel turn-off, two and a half hours had passed.

Why we travel with two vehicles
So there we were, at the foot of the Otto du Plessis Pass, faced by a slushy, muddy stretch of washed-away road. To one side were two high mud ridges with deep boggy trenches in-between, and a lot of squishy mud and water elsewhere, extending to a high bank. We made for the two ridges that looked the most solid, but the earth was so wet and slippery, the Freelander's wheels slid sideways and we lurched dangerously to one side as they sank into the trench. An elegant balletic curving slide (if my mouth hadn't been closed, my heart would have leapt right out) left us at a standstill, sideways, deep in thick, sucking, clay mud.⑤ Needless to say, packing rocks beneath the wheels gave them no traction. With the underside of the Freelander balancing on the high ridge, all four wheels were spinning in the thick muck (and coating the vehicle in even more slime).

With Keith some way behind us in the Hilux, out came the tow straps. Because Keith had to stay clear of the mess, it took two tow straps and one towrope tied together for him and his Hilux to haul the Freelander backwards, allowing Hirsh to straighten up the vehicle, with wheels lining up in the ruts. From there, using the Freelander's Mud and Ruts setting (similar to low range), he was able slowly and steadily to drive forward out of the mush.

Keith then ensured that he kept two wheels on the right-hand side of the bank, and he slowly and solidly pulled through.

This is why we **always** travel with two 4x4s …

Left onto R58 (direction Barkly East)

The road didn't improve, but with the mountains our guardians, a dazzling rainbow④ led us over successive river crossings and onto the tarred R58.

Barkly Pass (10–15 minutes)

This 13km tarred pass winds around the grassed mounds of the Drakensberg foothills, rising up and up, eventually carving into cracked and shattered rock at the topmost cliffs (1990m). The views are constantly surprising – onto pinched slopes, angled rocky promontories and rounded rock tops shaking off their grass toupees.⑥ There aren't obvious places to pull off and gaze at the patchwork of farmlands below, but with creative effort it's possible. Near the top, on the left, is Skilpad Rock – look for a rounded shell and an elongated neck and head. Gatberg is like a pimple on the top of a faraway hill with a tiny pinprick hole through it (it's in fact two rock slabs propping one another up).

Left off R58 to Mountain Shadows hotel

Expect no frills and furbelows at this hotel. Rows of little semi-detached rooms offer the absolute basics, and the food is standard hotel fare (canteen-style meat, vegetables, dessert). But the staff are very obliging and the owners personally greet you at meals, while advice asked for on local conditions is willingly given.

DAY 2
PASSES – BASTERVOETPAD, POTRIVIER, ELANDSHOOGTE, NAUDÉS' NEK

Mountain Shadows, detour to Bastervoetpad crest, then via three passes to Rhodes (231km)
Allow a full day for this leg

The mists and clouds had disappeared; it was a beautiful clear day. Leaving at 08:00 (we had a long day of passes ahead!), we took the gravel R393 directly across from the hotel.

The plan had been to do the Bastervoetpad all the way to Ugie, but due to rain, mud and road deterioration, our hotel host advised us to go as far as the crest, then retrace our steps – apparently the second half of the pass can be notoriously tricky. Looking back on it, we realised our host may have been overly cautious, but our own muddy rescue drill still so clear in our heads meant we were not open to unnecessary risks!

Bastervoetpad viewpoint (2 hours to crest and back; 39km)

These Eastern Cape mountains and valleys are marked by long, thin silhouettes of cypresses and Lombardy poplars, quite distinctive among the green-grassed hills and rock battlements. Before long a rusted signboard appeared for the pass (also named L.A.P.A. Munnik Pass after the former minister, but this name never stuck); we turned right here. As our 4x4s bumped over a stony, rutted, pitted road that had turned mushy and muddy in the rain, a Verreaux's (Black) Eagle twisted and turned beside us. In the distance two Grey Crowned Cranes were engaged in a mating dance, their enormous black-and-white underwings flapping furiously.

We crossed lots of babbling brooks and rose and fell across the foot of the slopes on a narrow track ⑦ very overgrown with grass tufts. Some heavily bouldered sections made it slow going, as we climbed steadily, chasing Grey-winged Francolins, and then three Cape Vultures and a Lammergeier! It was very exciting to see the glowing orange chest of the latter contrasting with those of the other vultures as they wheeled in the sky. It is sad that this is such a rare sighting.

When we got to the crest at 2247m, a wild wind was blowing. It felt as if we were on the roof of the world as we looked down on a panoply of riven emerald hills playing out to every horizon. It was all luminous-green peaks and valleys, cliffs and streams, the road forging a loopy path way below us

It felt as if we were on the roof of the world ...

91

⑦

🪧 **Left onto R396, through Maclear (follow Rhodes signs), continue on gravel for 63km**

Very potholed tar, then rutted gravel took us through pine plantations and on a long, circuitous route up to 1769m into a green mountain barricade that encircled us like a laager.

Potrivier Pass

After crossing a little bridge over a gurgling stream, the road does wide shallow loops around the base of a mountain slope. Keith's Hilux looked like a woolly mite on the track below. We rose directly level with the opposite upper slopes of a very narrow valley, the sharp deep V of the abyss separating us. At the crest we looked straight across at the slopes we'd just conquered; tilted ridges blocked out an azure-blue sky.

After the pass, we continued up and over pine plantations into an acid-green world. Herders carrying red hazard triangles regularly warned us of trooping cattle in the road.⑧ We constantly marvelled at the sight of cows acting like mountain goats in the highest mountain reaches.

Elandshoogte Pass

This pass kind of starts where you see the police station in the middle of nowhere – established to deal with cattle theft between nearby Lesotho's herders and local cattle owners. The eland that might have been here once upon a time are definitely no longer. The road climbs steadily through pine plantations and across grassed mountaintops, getting stonier and rockier as it goes.

🪧 **Take left fork to Rhodes (R396), continue for 41km**

Still on Elandshoogte, we were driving on a pretty good, recently graded road – up, down and around the mountains, above the plantations, with some short rocky sections to keep us on our toes. Only cattle shared the refined air with us.

Naudés' Nek

This dirt road, the highest in South Africa, clings to the edge of a massive mountain slope facing more massive slopes; you can see the track carving an angled cut-line across the opposite peak. With a few paltry bushes and upright stones to protect you along the road verge, the drop

... jigsaw-puzzle farmlands, all in blues, greens and browns ...

along the edge of the hills and then over and out of sight.

We would've loved to continue along the pass to Ugie, but plentiful rain, mud and caution won the day. Perhaps you'll be luckier, as it's a truly beautiful pass.

🪧 **Left onto R58 to Elliot (20km), left onto R56 via Ugie to Maclear (68km)**

Just a note for self-catering purposes: in spite of us being told otherwise, Elliot has a small Shoprite, and both Ugie and Maclear have a Spar (Ugie's is brand-new).

Who were the Basters?

The Bastervoetpad Pass got its name from a pioneering band of Griquas who, originally under the leadership of Adam Kok III, broke away during the trek of 1861/62 to today's Kokstad (then known as Niemandsland, or 'no man's land'). The trekking was characterised by drought, intense hardship and widespread loss of cattle. In efforts to forge a route over the mountains to the Ugie/Maclear area, wagons often had to be dismantled and carried across in pieces.

92

⑧

falls sheer to rounded hills in a very wide gentle faraway valley. A river cuts a thin, meandering, often obscured, path across the valley floor.

As the road zigzags up the slope, you start seeing packed-stone retaining walls, and here, just below the summit, is a wall with a heritage site plaque and space to pull off for a lunch or coffee stop.⑨ Which we did – lunch at this amazing spot was at 15:00.

Our GPS measured 2488m at the crest, so you can imagine the magnificence of the views: grass-matted humps and slopes, crests and valleys, jigsaw-puzzle farmlands, all in blues, greens and browns. It was two Naudé brothers ('*twee stoere boere*' quotes the monument located at the base of the pass) who got their horses to pick a trail over the mountain; they then built the pass (completed in 1911) using only picks, shovels and two-wheeled wooden carts.

We summited, then descended the *nek*, negotiating some washaways and embedded rock on an almost single-lane road.

Next was a series of dramatic loopy bends doubling back on themselves, the road weaving and wobbling as it went from one mountain spur to the next. It's here that an overcorrection or a slippery skid could take you on a precipitous tumble down a giant slope.

In the low-angled sun, the shadowed mountain fingers looked like brushed velvet. We bottomed out in a pastoral valley cupping a farmhouse set amidst tall Lombardy poplars. The road then meanders along the Bell River, sometimes suspended above it, as the mountains retreat slightly.

🪧 JUST BEFORE RHODES, TURN LEFT OFF R396 AT SIGN FOR KINMEL GUEST FARM AND LODGE

It had been a long day, and the appearance of our zinc-roofed self-catering cottage (Wilgerboom) with dormer windows facing the lower hills was a highly welcome one. Bedrooms and a bathroom are constructed in wood in the A-frame roof, and downstairs an open kitchen and lounge lead onto a long verandah with cane furnishings. The verandah looks out over a lawn and weeping willows on a stream bank. Our day was completed by the sight of a Verreaux's (Black) Eagle above us, evading harassment by smaller birds.

DAY 3
PASSES – CARLISLESHOEK, VOLUNTEERSHOEK, LUNDEAN'S NEK

Rhodes via three passes, Tiffindell and Wartrail to Lady Grey (168km) Allow a full day for this leg

The little village of Rhodes,⑩ signposted as a Proclaimed Conservation Area, is utterly charming. It is now what Greyton once was, before it attracted the hordes and became all sophisticated and popular. lined up at the foot of the Drakensberg and nestled beneath the drapery of countless weeping willows are tiny tin-roofed Victorian cottages with sash windows, *broekie*-lace and painted trim. No time to linger, though. There were heights to conquer and passes to slay.

🪧 OUT OF RHODES, DRIVE FOR 1KM (DIRECTION KINMEL), LEFT TO TIFFINDELL (21KM), CONTINUE TO WARTRAIL (26KM)

We started in fairly low grassed hills, passing farms and beautiful stylised weeping willows, just like in those Japanese paintings.

Carlisleshoek Pass to Tiffindell (1½ hours)

As the mountains loomed higher and higher, we were tracking a pebbled river along the foot of the hills, crossing many streams and winding through interlocking spurs. There were Lombardy poplars and a profusion of scarlet-berried sweetbriar, or *wilde roos*, which had trailed us throughout our mountain meanders; in summer its massed pink roses must look sensational along the roadside. Rising and descending – and avoiding cows and donkeys – we followed the road as it steepened, becoming stony and riven with gullies. Behind us, the mountain slopes formed serried rows.

Then a sign tells you to 'Engage lowest gear, drive confidently!' and you know you're in for trouble. Concrete strips, making the tightest turns imaginable, just keep on going up and up … this is no place to stall! When you're quite breathless, the road levels off and you can idle the vehicles a little, and get out to chant a calming *Om*. In the particularly steep section, we climbed just over 340m.

The second section, not as steep, nonetheless seriously deteriorates, with boulders and concrete fragments littering the centre. Luckily, a sign tells us: 'Only 10km to go. You've done the worst.'

At 2555m, we'd levelled off and were driving across a plateau, with Ben Macdhui, the Eastern Cape's highest peak (3000m), ahead. At this point you can see the defunct Tiffindell Resort (still tied up in legal wrangles) on the green slopes to the right at around 2700m. It's all a little sad, the deserted wooden chalets and ski lift with its skeletal seats running over the mountain crest. We passed Loch Ness Dam – looking neither very Scottish nor monsterish, although this is moorland-like country of tufted alpine grasses. A few Cape Vultures with splayed black wingtips were gliding quite low above us. We'd been on the road for an hour and a half.

Volunteershoek Pass (1½ hours)
This pass starts at the Loch Ness Dam. Up hill and down dale, we were still crossing the plateau, opening and closing farm gates, till we crested the summit at 2684m. Ahead on the skyline were some very high spiky peaks – the Malutis on the Lesotho border coming to meet the Drakensberg. Before long we were surrounded by peaks in shades of green, blue and purple. The perfect coffee stop (30°41'00.01"S, 27°52'32.21"E) at 2622m has you gazing onto an ocean of intersecting green hills, with layer upon layer stacking up behind. At the foot is the Wartrail valley. Then you descend on a twisty-turny track of stones, channels, dips and washaways. The slopes are weirdly speckled with cows – 'to be a cow in this part of the world, you've got to have a head for heights,' Hirsh observed. First gear and low range are a requisite

> ... stone-filled gullies and a loose pebbled surface had our wheels spitting out sharp stones ...

in places. No wrong moves can be made on a very steep rocky stretch with nothing but thin air beyond the gravel edge, and careful negotiation is required to get around a gigantic boulder sitting squarely on the road. A sharply angled, narrow, rutted, winding section left little room for manoeuvre, while stone-filled gullies and a loose pebbled surface had our wheels spitting out sharp stones. The descent itself took us half an hour.

Wartrail Valley
At the foot of the mountains, the Funnystone Farm buildings are followed by a dense grove of poplars that open up to black-streaked sandstone cliffs. Between two cliffs is a boulder-like protuberance supported by a thin neck of rock, the, um, funny stone. The valley runs

---

Warring in the Wartrail valley

During the time of the Great Trek, when new territories were being sought out and settled, inevitable conflicts arose between the Trekkers and indigenous peoples living in the area. The story goes that King Moshoeshoe I (or Moshesh), considered to be the first leader of the Basotho nation, would send bands of his followers across the Lesotho border to raid the Boers' cattle. The animals were herded across Moshesh's Ford on the Kraai River, then hustled up through Lundean's Nek into the mountain kingdom. Clashes arose as the Boers retaliated, and this is how the valley acquired its name.

Engage lowest gear, Keep up revs, ke corners wide, Drive confidently

parallel with the Funnystone River, and pretty shady clumps of trees are backed by striking rock walls. The name Wartrail has nothing to do with any assegai- or musket-fuelled battle; it's more to do with cattle marauders (*see* panel).

⚑ Turn right onto R393 (gravel), drive for 37km via Lundean's Nek to Telle River valley

I just loved the polished mountain domes with their patchy green toupees where the grass hadn't adhered to the smooth rock surface. Pin-tailed Whydahs floated across the road, black tail-banners fluttering after them.

Lundean's Nek (1¼ hours)

We were in a dragon's lair of crags and peaks and charcoal-stained cliffs, dwarfed by a towering barricade that all but closed us in. Ahead, the *nek* was discernible to the right of a trio of sharp rock pinnacles. But first we passed the local police station, specially established to deal with livestock thieves and dagga sellers trekking over from Lesotho. At the summit (2162m)⑫ the views were astounding. Ridge after ridge – near, middle and far – retreated to join the Malutis. As we rounded the corner we were suddenly in the midst of gigantic lime-green peaks pushing skywards, with massive rock boulders mushrooming out of the slopes. The entire skyline was blocked out by pinnacles and promontories.

Our vehicles nosed through and around and down the mountains, turning through switchbacks, bouncing through gullies, rattling over ridges, and avoiding serious washaways. Even in the belly of the mountains, the views were marvellous. Surprisingly, too, it was a toasty 32° – and we were way past midsummer (it was March)!

PLAN YOUR TRIP!

♦ **Web resources:**
Lady Grey: www.comfreycottage.co.za
Barkly Pass: www.mountainshadowshotel.co.za
Rhodes: www.kinmel.co.za
♦ Extra tourist resources and contacts: *see* pages 158–160

OUR EXPERIENCE

♦ **Best move on the trip:**
To ignore the traditional mealtime hours and rather base our coffee and lunch stops on the opportune moments in which a spectacular view presented itself – we really did experience some of the most memorable dining vistas in the country.

♦ **Worst move:**
Not pushing through to do the entire Bastervoetpad Pass, which is *truly* beautiful. As this little-used 4x4 pass is subject to rock falls and flooding after rainstorms, we took the advice of locals, but in retrospect we probably could have taken our chances.

♦ **Our advice to you:**
It's very important to listen to local knowledge, but understand too the advisor's unwillingness to take responsibility for any mishaps requiring trucks and tow-ropes! Bottom line: always **do** listen to local advice, exercise caution, and weigh up the personal consequences.

Telle River Valley

We were now trailing the Lesotho border in an open, flat valley ringed by mountains, passing little huts and settlements all the way. Then, *phisshh* … our second flat tyre of the trip. A sharp stone had cut straight through our tyre wall (yes, our tyres were overdue for replacement). Matters weren't helped much by a very rocky road cutting through a dense posse of hills.

⚑ Left onto gravel to Sterkspruit (36km), join R392 (tar) to Lady Grey (45km)

A stretch taking you past villages strung out at the foot of the lower Witteberg hills leads you back to your starting point, Lady Grey. From here, Aliwal North on the N6 connects to other national roads to get you back home. And having inhaled so much beauty in such a short time, you'll welcome the opportunity to simply catch your breath.

West-central Lesotho

Linear trip 454km starting Zastron, ending Wepener

What's so special about this route?
- The most stupendous mountainscapes this side of the Drakensberg escarpment
- Being privy to a life and pace that, in its simplicity, defies our rat-on-a-treadmill existence
- Until the Chinese road-builders have fulfilled their earth-heaving contract, Lesotho's roads are a nice test for your off-road skills (don't despair … there will always be the side roads and byways)

Trip summary
Features: Thin air and boundless vistas, rustic laid-back lodges, Basotho pony trekking
Trip duration: 5 days, 454km
Time of year: Mid-March (early autumn)
Linear trip: Zastron to Wepener
Road conditions: Potholed tar, stony gravel, some road erosion, rocky sections, ruts and washaways

Getting there (Zastron/Wepener)
(**Note:** travellers from Johannesburg or Durban should start their trip at Wepener/Van Rooyen's Hek border post, continuing to Mafeteng to join our route.)
From Johannesburg: N1 to Winburg, R709/R26 to Wepener
From Durban: N3 to Harrismith, N5 to Bethlehem, R26 to Wepener
From Port Elizabeth: N2 to East London, N6 to Rouxville, R26 to Zastron
From Cape Town: N1 to Gariep Dam, R701 to Smithfield, N6 to Rouxville, R726 to Zastron

MORE INFORMATION: **Plan Your Trip Info: page 107**
Tourist Resources: pages 158–160
MAPS: **This Route's Map: pages 98–99**
Also in Road Atlas Section: pages 150–156

West-central Lesotho

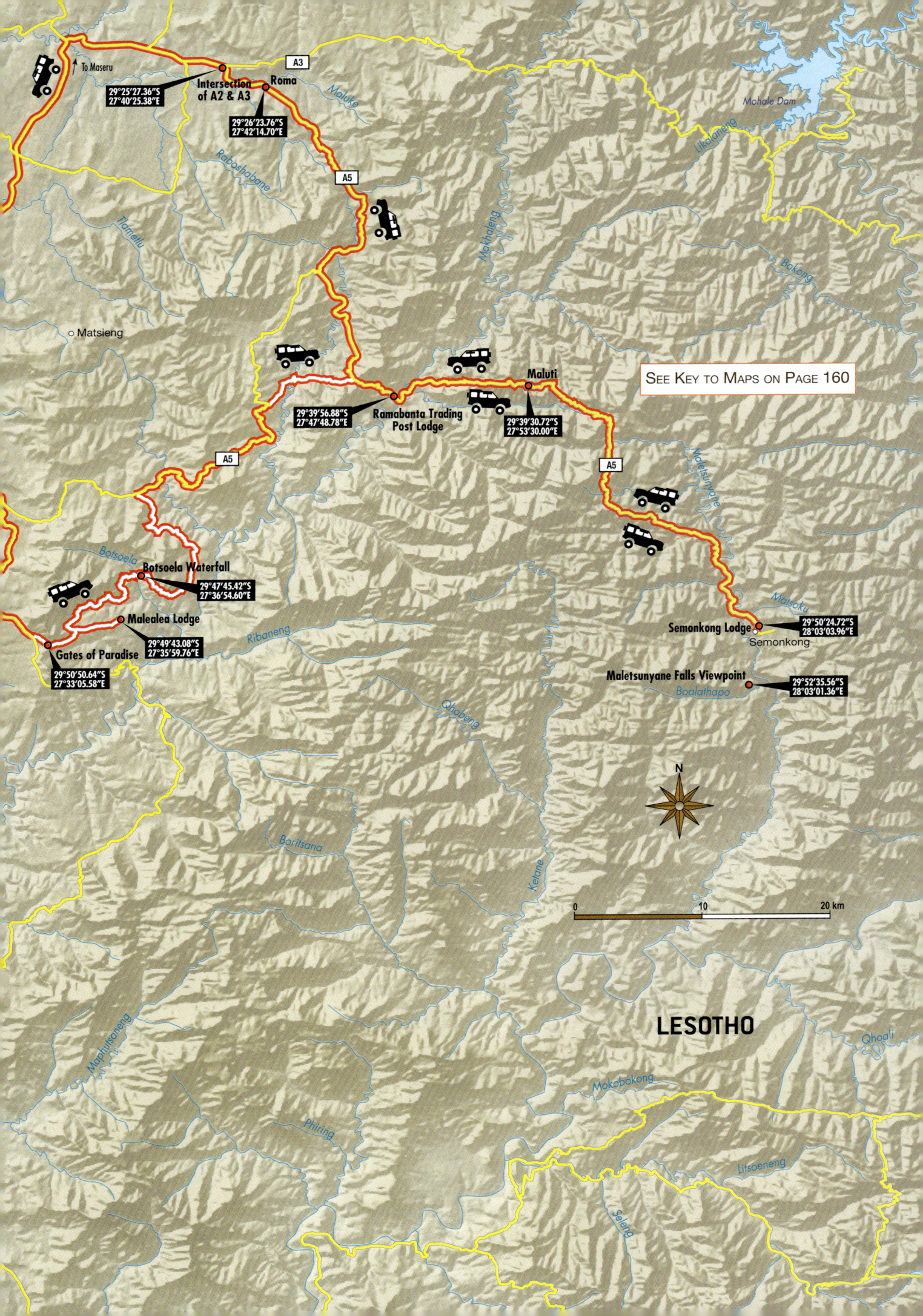

To Maseru	
Intersection of A2 & A3	29°25'27.36"S, 27°40'25.38"E
Roma	29°26'23.76"S, 27°42'14.70"E
Ramabanta Trading Post Lodge	29°39'56.88"S, 27°47'48.78"E
Maluti	29°39'30.72"S, 27°53'30.00"E
Botsoela Waterfall	29°47'45.42"S, 27°36'54.60"E
Malealea Lodge	29°49'43.08"S, 27°35'59.76"E
Gates of Paradise	29°50'50.64"S, 27°33'05.58"E
Semonkong Lodge	29°50'24.72"S, 28°03'03.96"E
Maletsunyane Falls Viewpoint	29°52'35.56"S, 28°03'01.36"E

See Key to Maps on Page 160

LESOTHO

DAY 1
Zastron via Makhaleng Bridge border post to Malealea Lodge (157km)
Leg time without stops: 3½ hours

After our Eastern Cape passes adventure, the three of us continued on to Lesotho, so we overnighted in Zastron, north of Lady Grey, beginning our new trip from there. Happily, we discovered Tienfontein Farm with its absolutely delightful 19th-century cottage (see panel, page 101).

Zastron itself is a one-horse town of line shops, offering the most basic amenities; it has one supermarket. Our plan to enter Lesotho via Van Rooyen's Hek was quickly revised after we were told a few times that the R26 to get there was heavily potholed … and also decidedly ugly. So Makhaleng Bridge it became.

⚑ Leave Zastron north, after 3km turn right onto R726, after 3km right onto flyover, left at stop street onto S2 (gravel) to Makhaleng bridge border post (37km)

Lombardy poplars accompanied us towards a blue Maluti-peaked skyline, as ridged hills rose steadily alongside us. We were amazed at the flocks of lipstick-hued Red Bishops and loved the Long-tailed Widowbirds with their red-and-buff shoulder patches and fluttery long tails.

Our passing through the tiny Makhaleng Bridge border post was effortless; ours were the only vehicles and the border officials seemed only too happy to see friendly new faces – it took us eight minutes max.

We paid a road toll tax and rumbled over an old rusty steel bridge spanning the Makhaleng River. Potholed tar took us through rounded hills and green grasslands to a junction.

⚑ Continue 4km, turn left onto A2, drive 4km to Mohale's Hoek, keep left on A2 to Mafeteng (47km)

A good tar road tracks the western Lesotho border, passing through countless settlements and villages and past maize fields, sheep and cattle – often ambling along verges and crossing the road – as well as crawling taxis (unusual!), which all seemed to be on a sightseeing mission, making our progress very slow. We were struck by the deeply eroded landscape, carved out by gullies, pits and troughs.

At the thriving little town of Mafeteng, we took the roundabout and left via the second exit on the A2.

⚑ Continue on A2 (26km) to Motsekuoa, turn right (direction Matelile), drive 24km, left onto gravel, drive 2km to Gates of Paradise

We certainly weren't going to collect any speeding fines with a speed limit that alternated constantly between 50 and 80kph. The tar deteriorated to potholes, and the telephone wires carried lots of Eastern Red-footed Falcons. As we headed inland, the enduring presence of dwellings,

> **Die Ou Huisie at Tienfontein**
> Die Ou Huisie, a self-catering cottage on Tienfontein Farm just southwest of Zastron in the Free State, is built of sandstone blocks and has a little *afdak* along one side facing onto a private garden. The cottage is lovingly furnished with yellowwood and stinkwood pieces, Voortrekker memorabilia, old framed posters and family photographs, enamelware and paraffin lamps. It comes with four-poster beds and starched linen, bird song and clear Free State air.
>
> Following our spate of punctures on the Eastern Cape passes, our helpful and friendly hosts put us in contact with a 24-hour tyre services person (Paul of Paul's Tyres, cell: 084 633 5135) – this at 18:30 on a Saturday evening – who pitched up a couple of hours later, took away our punctured tyres and returned them the same night. Service, indeed.
> Visit: www.safarinow.com/go/TienfonteinBandB

people and tiny thatched huts slowly dwindled, the valleys became emptier and the mountains more dominating as they edged towards us. Cultivated fields went on and on; agricultural terraces scaled even the mountain peaks. Among the wool-capped, blanketed herders, white gumboots were definitely in vogue (I discovered later that this is the symbol of a young initiate).

An eroded road rose to a *nek* at 2001m, signposted as the Gates of Paradise.③ We stopped to survey the landscape. The portal did open up to an expansive high-lying view onto an enormous flat cultivated valley② that's part of a series of plateaus contained by a collar of stacked spiky peaks. Known as Thaba Putsoa, they are the lower Malutis. From Hemel-op-Aarde to the Gates of Paradise … we were venturing into the hallowed portals of higher realms. If only we were as pure.

Continue on gravel for 6km to Malealea Lodge

From here a bumpy, unkempt road took us right into the heart of a village with chickens and goats and chatting villagers, to a scruffy reed fence beside little mud huts, horse troughs and reed shelters. Don't get a fright … this is the grand entrance to Malealea Lodge.

Malealea Lodge
The frayed fence is pulled aside and, under raggedy pine trees, you find a complex of thatched rondavels④ and little clay houses with blue zinc roofs, their walls decorated with pebbles and finger-painted geometric shapes. This place embodies the word 'rustic'. The huts and rondavels are clean but furnished with only the barest essentials – beds, a cupboard, a table fashioned out of beer cans. Yes, a little ingenuity has been harnessed here … right down to the kettle that is boiled (in 30 minutes) by attaching it to a gigantic silver saucer resembling a satellite dish in the garden. It stands outside the tiny coffee shop, a shanty with tables and chairs set among lawns and succulents. Look out for the exquisite spiral aloe; you'll know when you've found it. The main buildings, housing a cavernous, neglected and dusty entertainment room, a bar area, a dining room (plastic chairs and tablecloths) and a broad verandah, are all painted with colourful Lesotho characters and tableaux.⑤ The rooms and even some of the bathrooms, too, have bright murals. But everything has a gentle air of 'deconstructed' about it.

… a little ingenuity has been harnessed here …

To be honest, you kind of unwind and relax into these surroundings, and the big-hearted people running it will do everything they can for you. When we were there, Mick Jones was holding the fort for his daughter and son-in-law, who have taken over the reins but were having their annual break. Certainly, evenings on the verandah (only dinners are served at Malealea) are highly convivial and sociable, where you get to meet all kinds of travellers.

Malealea started out as a trading post, which explains its position at the village edge. We couldn't help thinking, though, that if just a teeny bit more upkeep went into, for example, the dodgy communal

That's where we were heading … off the edge of the plateau and into the abyss. And so began a steep, bouldery, sliding-stone descent through gullies and over shorn rocks, with the horse constantly having to find its footing. You've got to have faith – the animal stumbles often but quickly recovers (as Keith constantly reassured me, you can rely on the ponies' own strong sense of self-preservation).

But no sooner have you climbed down one mountainside, clipped your way along the edge of a river flowing over a rock shelf and crossed its waters, you're faced with the opposite vertiginous slope and a snaking switchback track that cuts its way straight up the mountainside. The most nerve-wracking bit was feeling the horse dip to gather its

… and then it was the heart-in-mouth descent …

back legs before leaping up onto the next ledge. At one point, the path was a mere thread on the cliff edge, where one slip of the pony's hoof would have had us both tumbling down the slope. Of course, as Mick Jones said, you can get off your trusty steed and walk at any time if the going gets too hairy.

But I have my pride …

In fact, the ponies are pretty docile save for breaking into an impromptu trot every now and again or pausing to lower their heads to snatch at the sweet grass. And so you rock and bounce and sway, at times leaning right back into the saddle, at others leaning forward to help your horse in a leap. The scenery is magnificent: vegetated crests, streaked cliffs and exposed ridges.

Eventually, at the top of the plateau, we dismounted and left our horses to rest and graze awhile, then hiked down a short, steep stony path to two lovely waterfalls, the Botsoela (meaning 'it spits'). The

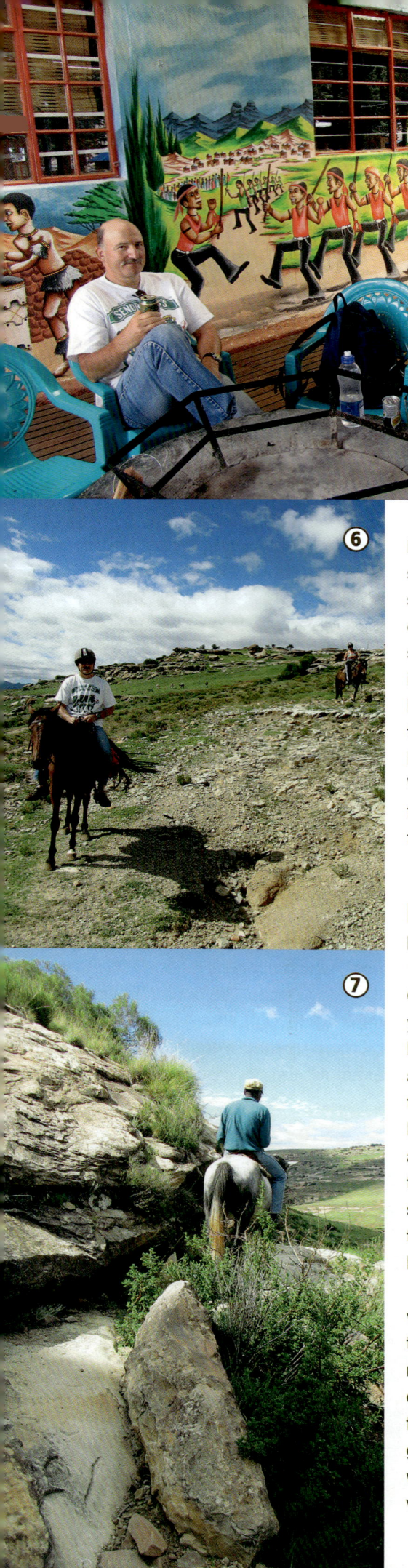

kitchen and furniture, the couple of shoddy bathrooms and the decor, such as the sad, faded photographs on the walls, it could be turned into something quite special. That said, it's a humming hub for overland tour buses and backpackers, who seem to love it just as it is (foreign travellers appear to enjoy its authenticity). Which is probably reason enough for the Jones family not to change their 'winning' formula.

DAY 2
Malealea – Basotho pony trek (2½–3 hours)

Other than a brief incident many years ago (when I fell off a steed galloping for home), I have never ridden a horse – but that's no reason not to experience a little excursion on Lesotho's amazingly agile national animal (well, it might as well be). So the three of us got kitted out, then saddled up and clip-clopped out of the gate on our gentle ponies led by Michael, our Basotho guide.⑦

After ambling through the village,⑥ the horses started picking their way over a smooth, buffed rocky plateau with only the tiniest eroded crevices for their hooves to find purchase. All around were ridged, green-grassed mountaintops – till we looked down into a bowl-like valley with mountain walls. Gulp.

one waterfall is a thin plume, the other a broader curtain flying some 40m over a cliff into a shallow, sandy pool surrounded by boulders. Of course, the ever-resourceful Lesotho locals had it all planned out: a small troupe of home-made-banjo-playing kids were waiting to sing and dance for us in expectation of a small fee.

Afterwards, we rode along the edge of the plateau with a different perspective over the waterfalls; then followed a heart-in-mouth descent and ascent to the opposite rock plateau along another route with its own challenges. I am filled with admiration for these incredibly sure-footed Basotho ponies. Considering the terrain, and us sitting on their backs like sacks of potatoes, they really do have their work cut out for them. Yet they're solid and steady and strong.

Sunset Drive

After a self-catered lunch in the garden and a leisurely afternoon, we drove, under heavy dark clouds, on a badly washed-away road onto a high plateau till our track ran out. Here you understand the term 'mountain kingdom'① because everywhere you look are giant landscapes of peaks and Lesotho-hat-like hills. We could see glimpses of the river we'd tracked, and the impossibly high cultivated terraces, huts and herders. Everywhere we went, we were followed by excited little kids.

DAY 3
Malealea Lodge to Semonkong Lodge (110km)

On our way out of Malealea we passed, in the fields, dramatic-looking birds with red bulbous heads, thin-curved beaks and iridescent plumage. They turned out to be Southern Bald Ibis.

LEAVE MALEALEA VILLAGE, TURN RIGHT AND DRIVE ON GRAVEL FOR 31KM

Travelling on a very rutted, stony road, we stayed in the valley, traversing the lower hill slopes and crossing plenty of streams. Peach trees were growing wild everywhere; intrigued, we stopped to pick a couple of their fruits. Some peaches were intensely sweet – wonderful bounty for the local villagers, we thought.

We were steadily rising, skirting the left-hand wall of the huge valley bowl but never ranging far from mountain villages, some of the shanties sporting a satellite dish on the roof – a bewildering mix of rural simplicity and technology. A row of hairpin bends took us into the valley again, as we contemplated the track zigzagging up to the opposite crest. Two schoolboys, agile as goats, raced down the mountain, with flailing arms and much ululating, taking short cuts and twists and turns in an effort to beat us to the bottom.

Our 4x4s made slow progress, rocking up the opposite slopes lined with sagewood, *ouhout* and sweetbriar. The road levelled out, skirting the mountain edge, then cresting. Here, on the right, was space to park and a pathway to a high point from which you gaze into two valleys, one to either side of the mountain you've just crossed.

⚑ **At a three-road fork, bear right, continue for 27km**

And so we continued, descending one mountain and ascending the next: on the horizon a crinkled skyline all the way from west to east, montane grassland plateaus looking onto terraced valleys and maize fields⑧ – this under an intense blue sky and in 30°C temperatures. We were struck by how electric-green the mountains were; the last time we'd travelled to Lesotho, it was just after winter and the hills were all russet-brown.

In spite of the heat, herders were clad in their blankets and initiates wore their white gumboots proudly.

We passed two very unusual pimpled peaks, then we were winding up a mountain on a bad, steep, narrow track that was also rocky, pitted and washed away. It, in fact, became a very well-surfaced road where it had been rolled flat in roadworks that were still under way.

⚑ **At T-junction, turn right onto A5, continue 4km to Ramabanta Trading Post Lodge**

We were heading for Ramabanta Trading Post Lodge (at Malealea's suggestion), where we hoped to persuade them to ply us with lunch. The well-graded road continued; huge drifts of pink and white cosmos greeted us from the valleys. We were now in the Malutis proper, at a height of 2000m. After coming over a *nek* that gave on to 180° views of peaks spread before us, we took a left turn to Ramabanta village.

... past villagers and ponies and herders ...

The Trading Post Lodge, a collection of thatched sandstone cottages on a sloping plateau with great views onto the Malutis, had humble beginnings too, as its name suggests. The place was dead quiet, but the lady on duty didn't bat an eyelid at offering us toasted cheese sandwiches – which we gratefully accepted and munched under the trees on the lodge lawns, a cool breeze making it entirely pleasant. The Makhaleng River followed a twisted course below.

⚑ **Exit left onto A5, continue to Semonkong Lodge (48km)**

Then on we went, climbing up and up, through groups of huts and past villagers, ponies, herders (one in woollen cap and blanket checking his cellphone), terraced and grassed mounds and, increasingly, over rocky mountains.

At the crest of a high mountain, a funny rusted sign was almost illegible due to the proliferation of bullet holes piercing the metal. Now we really were on the roof of Lesotho, a sea of rounded mounts rising and dipping beneath us and broad, shallow rivers winding through the valleys.⑨

Negotiating the pits and ruts and stones of the road, we travelled under the silent, watchful gaze of countless herders, here wearing bizarre long, funnelled hats straight out of the Wizard of Oz. Near the top of one particularly steep incline, we encountered an old bakkie stuck in the middle of the road. It took much conferral and inspection of the road shoulders before Keith slowly edged past the vehicle, his wheels perilously close to the sheer drop-off. Then out came the tow strap to haul the driver and his passenger over the crest to the next village. Grinning broadly, they couldn't believe their luck.

At Semonkong, again a sprawling village acts as a gateway to the lodge. A very steep, rocky, bouncy road took us down to a bridge over the Maletsunyane River, across which, at the foot of high cliffs, is the lodge complex. The drive from Malealea had taken us seven hours.

⑩

Semonkong Lodge

Yes, it was once a trading post ... and the fun element here is that the road sandwiched between lodge and river-cliff is a busy thoroughfare that links a string of villages, so there is constant traffic of cattle and sheep being herded, blanketed men on Basotho ponies, donkeys laden with sacks of mealie meal, and villagers on foot.

The lodge is definitely a step up in luxury: the stone-and-thatch rooms (some freestanding, some attached) feature handcrafted wood-and-reed cupboards, good linen, benches with pretty cushions, wool rugs, and original oil paintings by local artists. There is even a wood fireplace for frostier temperatures. The main buildings, with kitchen, bar (Thatchers Tavern), dining room and a little open terrace facing the cliff, have also been done with care. Wood-and-steel dining chairs, fabric tablecloths, tiny vases with fresh flowers, a long bench crammed with cushions all make it intimate and inviting. The charm, we decided, lies in the details.

The menu, too, is much classier than we'd expected, with a choice of dishes in three courses – I was even served smoked salmon in the remote, inaccessible depths of central Lesotho!

Keith and I were totally charmed when we discovered that the British royal princes had stayed here on their charity stints in Lesotho – Keith had Harry's room and Hirsh and I were in William's! I couldn't help thinking of Prince William sitting on the bed, gazing at the same painting as I was, and revelling in the fleeting freedom of this life so far removed from the pomp and ceremony of his own kingdom.

DAY 4
Maletsunyane Falls and Sundowner Route (directions from Semonkong Lodge)

Semonkong means 'place of smoke' – which refers to the fine mist and spray swirling in the air around the Maletsunyane Falls, a three-quarter-hour drive from the lodge. And this is where we were headed after breakfast.

Maletsunyane Falls (22km, two-hour round trip)

We passed through Semonkong village, easing over a washed-away road across an open grassed valley encircled by rounded hills.⑪ Southern Red Bishops and Long-tailed Widowbirds entertained us in the cornfields. After passing through a gate, we climbed a mountain to a second valley of hills and huts and herders, negotiating steep, eroded ascents and descents.

The vehicles climbed a rise and we were suddenly face to face with a row of sheer basalt cliffs⑬ plummeting into a deep, narrow cleft cutting across the earth like a scar. (You're so high up in this part of the world that the rock still consists of outpourings of resistant ancient lava – the topmost layer of the Drakensberg range.) We bounced along the grassland plateau on a rutted and muddy, heavily grassed track to the lookout point.

The plateau steps down a couple of times to the gorge edge, where above you the river shoots over an exposed rock lip between enormous craggy cliffs,⑫ fanning out into a lace web just above the pool. The sound of the falls slapping the river

MALETSUNYANE FALLS ←

somewhere along this stretch of road, we were told, we'd see the extensive roadworks being carried out by the Chinese, who seem to be infiltrating Africa wherever we look.

A rather bumpy embedded-stone road led us up and over, down and up, over and down one mountain after another.

We reached an elevation of 2550m from where we looked onto cultivated valleys⑩ with subsistence crops of wheat, mealies, potatoes and sunflowers⑭ in squares of green, yellow and mushroom-brown. On mountain terraces, golden wheat had been cut and stacked into little conical-hat heaps. Mounted herdsmen looked like tiny model figurines.

After a steep, muddy river crossing we rose even further to 2620m, getting a mesmerising 180° panorama: layers of Maluti hills, from green and rounded to pinched and peaked purple. You could see to the other end of the world. These views definitely topped any we'd seen thus far on our mountain and pass tour.

When we did eventually get to the 'end of the road' at our roadworks base, there wasn't a single Chinese hat in sight. It was the end of the day, of course, but we felt slightly cheated.

That evening we watched big-winged Southern Bald Ibises coming in to roost on the basalt cliff opposite the lodge; the proprietors of Semonkong Lodge told us that at one time there were up to 300 birds breeding and roosting on these cliffs.

below is like that of waves crashing to the shore. The drop of 186m counts among Africa's highest single-drop falls, but it's difficult to get a sense of perspective, as here, everything is so grand in size. The waterfall certainly wasn't at its prime, and the cliff is south-facing, so it's always in shadow but lovely nonetheless. To either side of the tumbling water, rock fingers break away in fitful peaks and pillars separated by grass clefts. I watched a Jackal Buzzard – the first raptor in days – cruising the air currents over the gorge.

You can drive further, through the grasses, on a semblance of a rough track to the plateau edge to look down onto the gorge and a tight loop of the river before backtracking to Semonkong.

Sundowner Route (round trip: 1½ hours)

We followed a road out of the village, eventually heading south-east towards the Senqunyana (Little Orange) River; at a junction

DAY 5
Semonkong Lodge via Roma and Van Rooyen's Hek border post to Wepener (187km)

⚐ Exit Semonkong on A5, continue via Ramabanta (47km) to Roma (36km)

It struck us that when you're in central Lesotho you spend more time dodging goats, sheep and cattle than you do vehicles (that in itself carries its own charm).

We retraced our steps to Ramabanta village, gaining a different perspective on the mountainscapes while descending 1000m in altitude.

Although still encircled by the Malutis, we were back to Golden Gate-style buff sandstone cliffs with charcoal streaks and grass matting. Running first along the top of the sandstone plateau, watching the land fall away to deep valleys with boulders and freestanding pillars, we were soon at the foot of it, driving beneath scoured overhangs.

After passing a bustling Roma village, the mountains retreated to the horizon and we were back in densely inhabited territory.

⚐ Continue through Roma on A5 for 5km, left onto A3, drive 12km, left onto A2 to Mafeteng (62km)

A succession of villages, grasslands and mountain ridges along our right took us into Mafeteng.

⚐ At Mafeteng roundabout take 4th exit via Van Rooyen's Hek border post (17km) to Wepener (8km)

It took us four hours to reach the border at Lesotho's western boundary. And it took us all of one minute to re-enter South Africa. The border-post staff were so disinterested, they hardly raised their eyes from whatever deep conversation they were engaged in. Pity we have no record of ever having left Lesotho … uh-oh, the police are banging down our front door. Gotta go …

PS – From Wepener, the R702 meets up with the N1, N6 and N8 at Bloemfontein; the R26 travels south towards Aliwal North and the N6.

Mounted herdsmen looked like tiny model figurines …

PLAN YOUR TRIP!

♦ **Web resources:**
Tienfontein Farm, Zastron:
www.safarinow.com/go/TienfonteinBandB
Malealea Lodge:
www.malealea.co.ls
Ramabanta Trading Post Lodge:
www.tradingpost.co.za
Semonkong:
www.placeofsmoke.co.ls

♦ Extra tourist resources and contacts: *see* pages 158–160

OUR EXPERIENCE

♦ **Best move on the trip:**
Carrying a spare tyre in addition to our spare wheel; the fact is, although a tyre can always be patched (even if only temporarily), it's not always that easy to find the right *size* tyre – and that doesn't apply only when you're in the *gramadoelas*!

♦ **Worst move:**
This would have been a 'worst move' had we not heeded local advice. Don't make the mistake of going through Lesotho's busiest border post at Maseru; you could be faced with lines and lines of locals travelling to and from their places of work to either side of the border. The smaller border crossings we chose were an absolute breeze; we even had officials coming to the vehicle to check our documents for us!

♦ **Our advice to you:**
Don't take the tyre advice lightly: in terms of lethal sharp-edged stones, the roads we travelled on throughout Lesotho were consistently bad, some even worse than the devilish Richtersveld roads we'd been so hotly warned about.

Kgalagadi's wilderness camps

Round trip
250km
starting/ending
Upington

What's so special about this route?

- First, a warning! You'll hear all the tales of lion, cheetah and leopard encounters but ... stay long enough, and *you'll* be telling the tales!
- If true remote wilderness is what you're looking for, Kgalagadi has it in heaps
- Such ingenuity has been applied to the architecture of the wilderness camps, it's a shame not to put them to the test

Trip summary

Features: Wilderness camps with flush toilets, hot showers and oodles of class, dune driving, exhilarating big-cat sightings
Trip duration: 10 days, 250km
Time of year: Early May (autumn)
Round trip: Starting and ending in Upington
Road conditions: Heavy corrugations, stony, very sandy, *middelmannetjies* with high grass and seeds, steep sand ascents and descents

Getting there (Upington)

From Johannesburg: N1/N14 to Upington
From Durban: N3/N5 to Winburg, N1 to Bloemfontein, N8 to Kimberley, R64 to Groblershoop, N10 to Upington
From Port Elizabeth: N2/N10 to Upington
From Cape Town: N7/N14 to Upington

MORE INFORMATION: **Plan Your Trip Info: page 121**
Tourist Resources: pages 158–160
MAPS: **This Route's Map: pages 110–111**
Also in Road Atlas Section: pages 150–156

Kgalagadi's wilderness camps

Mabuasehube Area

BOTSWANA

Kgalagadi Transfrontier Park

See Key to Maps on Page 160

NAMIBIA

- Gharagab Trail Start (One Way)
- Grootkolk Wilderness Camp — 25°01'55.47"S 20°18'49.57"E
- Gharagab Wilderness Camp — 24°48'03.68"S 20°01'25.84"E
- To Union's End
- Gharagab Trail End
- Nossob Camp
- Bitterpan Trail Start (One Way) — 25°25'18.03"S 20°35'47.30"E
- Bitterpan Camp — 25°42'58.33"S 20°24'12.98"E
- Dikbaardskolk Picnic Site — 25°46'14.86"S 20°43'48.44"E
- Kamqua Picnic Site — 26°01'24.03"S 20°24'18.83"E
- Urikaruus Wilderness Camp — 26°00'36.18"S 20°20'57.63"E
- Kieliekrankie Camp — 26°11'01.16"S 20°35'31.54"E
- Rooiputs
- Twee Rivieren Camp — 26°28'23.01"S 20°37'02.22"E
- Twee Rivieren Border Post
- Strathmore — 25°48'23.54"S 20°06'13.03"E
- Kalahari Tented Camp — 25°52'00.78"S
- Bitterpan Trail End
- Mata Mata Border Post — 25°47'08.79"S 20°01'04.40"E
- Mata Mata Camp

Nossob

Auob

110

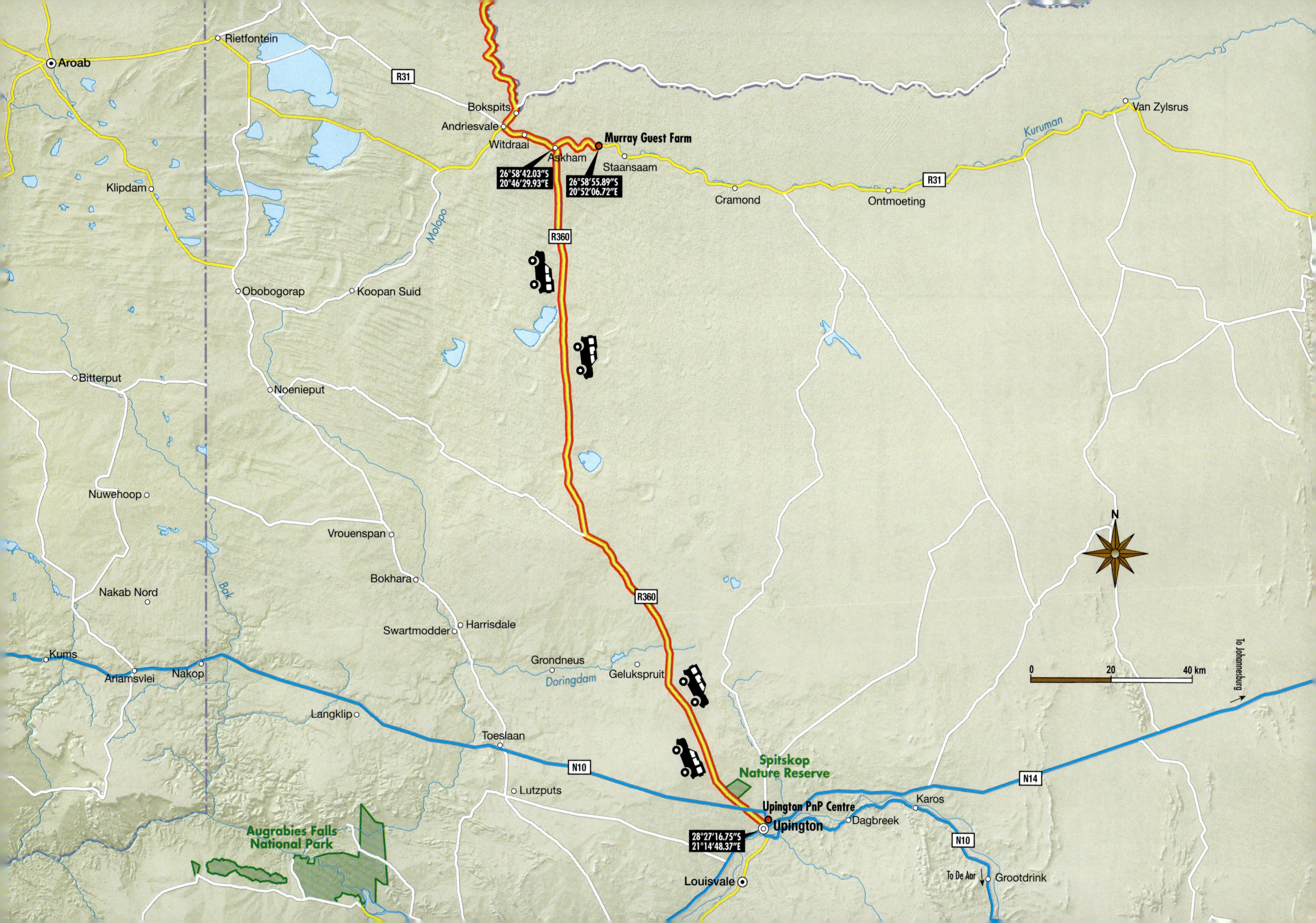

Aroab
Rietfontein
R31
Bokspits
Andriesvale
Witdraai
Askham
Murray Guest Farm
Staansaam
26°58'42.03"S
20°46'29.93"E
26°58'55.89"S
20°52'06.72"E
Cramond
Ontmoeting
Van Zylsrus
Kuruman
Klipdam
Molopo
R360
Obobogorap
Koopan Suid
Bitterput
Noenieput
Nuwehoop
Vrouenspan
Bokhara
Nakab Nord
Bak
Swartmodder
Harrisdale
Kums
Ariamsvlei
Nakop
Grondneus
Doringdam
Gelukspruit
Langklip
Toeslaan
N10
Lutzputs
Spitskop
Nature Reserve
Upington PnP Centre
Upington
28°27'16.75"S
21°14'48.37"E
Dagbreek
Karos
N14
Augrabies Falls
National Park
Louisvale
To De Aar
Grootdrink
N
0
20
40 km
To Johannesburg

DAY 1
Getting to Kgalagadi

Full disclosure upfront: this trip is a revisit of Kgalagadi, our original exploits already committed to print in the first book, *Our Top 4x4 Trips*. Our first foray into the Kalahari, however, was so brief, our experiences in only two wilderness camps so limited, we felt we simply hadn't done the park justice. So, this time around, the plan was to stay *only* in the unfenced wilderness camps, using Nossob in the centre of the park as a way station between the extreme north and south.

🕇 Leave Upington on R360 (tar), drive 275km to Kgalagadi Transfrontier Park

From Upington, the R360 shoots due north (with a little dogleg) to the southernmost tip of the transfrontier park, where the bustling-railway-station camp, Twee Rivieren, ushers you into the depths of the wild Kalahari dune lands.

Most travellers will come from afar, and will need to overnight somewhere before starting their exploring. Instead of Twee Rivieren, we chose Murray Guest Farm, near Askham, 84km outside Kgalagadi (*see* panel, this page).

DAY 2
To Kieliekrankie Camp
Route

After our overnight stop, we had the entire day to make our way to our first wilderness camp. From Twee Rivieren, two dry riverbeds – the Auob and Nossob – forge dual game-viewing routes, like a loose-limbed V, up through the Kgalagadi on the South African side (the Nossob is, in fact, the dividing line between South Africa and Botswana). Very rarely does the water flow here, and then only after particularly prolific rains. The pair of roads track, cross and, at times, even run along the centre of each riverbed.

The Auob, the left-hand arm, which right now is drawing our vehicles up towards Kieliekrankie, is narrower, and more contained, than the Nossob. It's also flat and heavily grassed. The road, though, is badly corrugated, our wheels chewing and spitting out stones

---

Murray Guest Farm

Murray Guest Farm, 12km east of Askham, is just 84km from Kgalagadi, so it's ideally placed for long-distance travellers needing an overnight stop before entering the park. The 'cottages' are four dinky flat-roofed brick units kitted out with the barest necessities, yet they're nicely done. Each one has an iron four-poster bed and white embroidered linen in one bedroom, primary-colour single beds in another, a rain shower-head in a minuscule new bathroom, a tiny lounge, and a basic kitchen. But the main activity happens outside at the bricked braai area, in the midst of Kalahari thornveld and camel-thorn trees.

There is also a 'field camp': a reed camp for eight people with a communal kitchen, no electricity.
Visit: www.murrayguestfarm.co.za

as we go. To get to the camp, we traverse part of the link road that connects the Auob with the Nossob, crossing the wilder parts of Kgalagadi. Rolling brick-red dunes are held together by seeded tufts and rippling grasses, golden and supple as the mane of a lion.

The herds you know are going to be there because they thrive in the openness and flatness of the sand channels are indeed present: gemsbok wielding lethal horns,② springbok, red hartebeest and heavy-headed wildebeest. The anthills, though, are deceptive. Keith laments, 'I keep on seeing lions.' Hirsh shoots back, 'I'm told if you dream long and hard enough, your dreams turn into reality.' We all chuckle.

Camp details
A special feature of the wilderness camps is that they never exceed four units – a whiff of exclusivity, to be sure – and are unfenced. There are also some camps that lie at the end of dedicated 4x4 roads, as if in the middle of nowhere.

Kieliekrankie's four cubes,① in shades of rust and khaki, guard the crest of a dune, their cantilevered wood-and-reed decks offering 180° vistas. Part plastered brick, part canvas walls, the units' facilities are tastefully done. A wavy landscape of camel-thorns, yellow grasses and grey-mound bushes stretches to infinity. Way below is a tiny pumped water hole that's lit up at night.

Highlight
We sigh with pure pleasure at hearing the sounds of yipping black-backed jackal, the first of our trip, and the high-pitched '*scree*' of a Barn Owl (later, the sail-like flutter of white wings alerts us to an owl attending to its bath-time ritual at the water hole). Some time later, picking up movement, we train our binoculars on an African wild cat slinking about within the spotlight's beam.

But our real highlight happens the next morning when, shortly after leaving camp, we chance upon a foraging honey badger.③ Closely trailed by two Pale Chanting Goshawks (known to hover for small prey flushed out by the badgers), the creature pads hyperactively from hole to hole, snuffling the red earth and digging wildly with sand radiating in all directions. At times, only his black butt protrudes from a hole. Next, he makes a beeline for a tree with low-hanging branches. To our amazement, he climbs it, scrabbling at the bark, then biffs something to the ground as the goshawks flutter on the outskirts. We're elated at such a prime sighting because honey badgers are generally nocturnal.

DAY 3
To Kalahari Tented Camp
Route
On the map, Kalahari Tented Camp⑧ (together with nearby Mata Mata) pegs the end of the dry Auob riverbed to the Namibian border. Our slow trundle up the Auob is constantly interrupted by raptors on the wing (Tawny and Snake-Eagles), raptors keeping rigid-backed sentry (Gabar and Pale Chanting Goshawks), and smaller, daintier ones peering prettily from dead branches (Pygmy④ and Lanner Falcons). It must have been my pronunciation of Gabar, but Keith's radio response is, 'Goshawks at the gay bar?' We fall about laughing. Raptors (Cape and White-backed Vultures) fiercely adjudicate from giant nests sprouting out of camel-thorn crowns. We are alerted by other travellers to a male lion, stretched out and comatose, on the far side of the Auob. He's so soporific we can't quite muster any enthusiasm.

When we stop for a coffee break, the toilet facilities at the Kamqua Picnic Site (which are few and far between) definitely get my vote. Nearing Mata Mata, the dunes maintain a bulkier swagger and glow richly russet. Grasses both on the slopes and in the riverbed are thick and lustrous. We also say hello to our first giraffes,

Rolling brick-red dunes are held together by seeded tufts and rippling grasses ...

with their crazy-paving coats and Maybelline-length eyelashes.

Camp details
I love this camp, although it's the only one to have 15 units versus the normal four. Still, the 'tents' – constructed of stacked sandbags, sealed and painted – are well spaced and private. With their wooden floors and deck, canvas roof and walls, and ceiling fans, they exude the atmosphere of an elegant old-time safari. A separate tent serves as a kitchenette and dining area. The camp – ranged on a dune above the dry Auob, which is cut by a long, thin sliver of a water hole – faces the opposite high bank down which antelope and night prowlers descend. In the late afternoon, a large herd of springbok, a lone wildebeest and a few gemsbok dawdle in the riverbed.

Highlight
The night sky ⑤ is brittle and beautiful, the tightly arranged stars of the Milky Way glittering like marcasite. Pity then that the failing spotlight sputters forth such a weak glow, the water hole remains cloaked in darkness. We do, though, eavesdrop on a pair of jackals calling back and forth to each other immediately below us. And in the depths of the night, we're treated to a resounding orchestra of *'whoo-oop, whoop, whoop'* from spotted hyenas, followed by a chorus of yowling, whinnying jackals. In-between, like the sobering notes of a bass, are the throaty grunts of an antelope – or is it a wildebeest?

DAY 4
To Nossob Camp
Route
Rising the next morning, we can't feel our fingers and toes. It's 7°C. Today we're headed for Nossob. Although Urikaruus Wilderness Camp is just down the drag, reaching it makes too short a day for us, as we need to get to Gharagab, which lies at the end point of the park on the Nossob. Meanwhile, Nossob Camp provides a good waypoint at the halfway mark of the river route. (Urikaruus … we'll get back to you!)

We head for the link road connecting to the Nossob River, and at Kamqua Picnic Site we find 12 giraffe circled round a low green outcrop, their sinuous necks curved in synchrony. Then we see another, and another … several more … ⑥ Eventually we count 20.

Good thing, since the two crossroads – cutting through an ocean swell of dunes pegged in place by sun-golden grasses and *driedoring*

Don't leave behind …
♦ Drinking water: all the wilderness camps request that you bring your own. For an eight-day trip, we had 80 litres of drinking water (1 x 40-litre, 2 x 20-litre tanks); better safe than sorry.
♦ Garbage bags: to use as bin liners; most camps don't supply these in internal dustbins, only in external braai bins. Also, at picnic spots you need to take out whatever you bring in.

(wild pomegranate) bushes – seldom deliver more than solitary gemsbok, dusty ostriches and rosy-legged goshawks. That's not to say, though, that you can't come face to face with a giant cat padding through …

Up-down, up-down (by now it's 11:00 and 29°C), we get to Dikbaardskolk Picnic Site on the Nossob. On our last trip to Kgalagadi, I praised its facilities. This time, they're not so good – but we're aware of a drastic water shortage in Nossob. Many of the water holes, too, are dry; sometimes it's the pumps that are out of order. It's a constant reminder that we're in true wilderness where rain and water are doled out grudgingly. Here it really *is* survival of the fittest.

The Nossob riverbed is very broad, in places bare and sandy, in others covered with stunted bushes and sizable spreading camel-thorns. But, unlike the Auob, it also has high, grassed banks alongside the road, which tend to obscure game-viewing.

Camp details
Note: Nossob is not a wilderness camp. Its painted brick chalets, attached in pairs, are simple and basic, some decorated with San-style wall hangings of quills, seeds and pods. In our chalet, we notice that one of the hangings has had all its porcupine quills neatly removed by some conscience-less pilferer, leaving only the hessian cloth behind. *Some people!*

Highlight
The thing about Nossob is it has a well-lit water hole closely guarded by a wooden hide that appears to attract all manner of unexpected guests, despite its position adjacent to the camp's entry road. Earlier in the evening, we watched a black-backed jackal trying to snap a dove in mid-air, as a flock descended and rose from the water in a whirring cloud – but nothing more. Then, way into the night, the deep, throaty rumble and descending grunts of a lion have us wide-eyed and primed for action. The first call sounds really close. Subsequent roars, at well-spaced intervals, become increasingly distant.

The next morning, as we're driving out of the gate, a couple of kilometres on, on the opposite bank of the river, is a shaggy-maned male lion making his way towards the camp.

The night sky is brittle and beautiful …

Several 4x4s, ours among them, do a swift U-turn and race back to the water hole where we all collect in the creaking hide. A hush settles, pregnant with promise; the only sound is our breathing. And, yes, the beautiful male,⑦ whom we notice is limping badly, heads our way. He stops and starts, stops and starts, taut as a guitar string, intensely alert. He overshoots the water, then guardedly turns back. Slowly, slowly, the lion approaches the water hole, nervy and twitchy, each step measured. The clicking of cameras rips the silence like firecrackers. He raises amber eyes in a penetrating gaze, but it's the firing of a vehicle's engine nearby that has him wheel round and bound off up the riverbed.

DAY 5
To Gharagab Wilderness Camp
Route
Today we're heading north. But not too far south of Nossob is a meandering circular detour, Marie se Draai, where regular sightings of lion and cheetah occur. We first take a *draai* here (see Highlight, page 116), before backtracking to the north.

The Nossob is a sea of yellow grass, but camel-thorns also hold sway, dominating the sands, the savannah, the dunes. Their trunks are a marvel of tree architecture, wound and twisted, their bark so crusty they resemble the fat, frayed ropes of an old sailing ship. And their beautiful half-moon pods continue to bewitch me.

Temperatures are back to 30°C, raptors are planing – Steppe Buzzard, Tawny Eagle and Bateleur, the latter's scarlet legs and undertail bright as a red tail-light.

We detour to a water hole and find a Tawny Eagle, an African Harrier Hawk and a trio of long-legged Secretary Birds in their black britches, all sharing the same space. The Harrier Hawk glides down towards the water but, with a flurry of extended wings and shivering quill feathers, a Secretary Bird confronts it. A thin, mincing kick in mid-air delivers a hefty blow to the hawk and a feathered fracas ensues, till the hawk retreats in defeat. Next, there's a confrontation between the Tawny Eagle and another raptor that's joined the fray, with much aerial acrobatics and evasive tactics being displayed. We're speechless that at 14:00 in shimmering heat we're privy to so much action.

The 32km one-way track to Gharagab ⑨ is very sandy, with sharp twists and dips and rises. We're way off the main route now, in true wild Kalahari, where nothing but ostriches and a jackal stir. The soil is orange-red, like oxidised iron. Later, tight corrugations make the going bumpy and a high *middelmannetjie* is thick with grass seeds (our nets are secured in place).

Camp details
At Gharagab (meaning 'house of the old Hottentot captain' – don't ask) four reed-and-canvas units, ⑩ with wooden floors and front decks, are raised on low poles. Inside each is a tiny kitchenette and, beyond, two beds backed by a small hanging cupboard, followed by a shower/toilet. The cabins stand on the edge of a deep, narrow valley at the foot of which is a tiny water hole. Frustratingly, the spotlight here is also out of commission; the camp manager is struggling to find the problem.

Highlight
Big cats: they're one of the singularly most hair-tearing elements of Kgalagadi. Since all three of these lithe creatures are magnetically drawn to Kgalagadi's flat open grasslands, you are constantly bombarded by reports of travellers who had just spent an hour watching lion cubs at play, or had a cheetah slope over the road in front of them, or had caught sight of a leopard at dusk lapping at a water hole. The truth is, such moments are ephemeral; one minute a creature is there, the next it has become one with the grasses. It's a story of split-second timing, hitting a site at precisely the right moment. Often there's disappointment. And yet … one day the lucky dice roll into *your* corner. Last trip, we lost out. Today lady luck is hanging around.

The occupants of a number of stationary vehicles alert us to cheetah in the grasses. With much focus we make

116

out two dark heads framed by sun-backed grass. They're sitting still, alert, backs to us as they watch a nearby herd of springbok wandering by, clueless to the danger just a single *pronk* away. One of the cheetahs suddenly breaks cover. With a panicked snort, a young springbok bolts like an arrow released from an archer's bow. What follows is utterly thrilling. The cheetah gathers speed, easing gracefully into her stride. We see her streaking through the grasses, body taut and muscled yet streamlined, elongated. Supremely elegant, every muscle working in harmony, she moves at a speed that's breathtaking. It's sheer poetry to watch. It seems as if the springbok's fate is sealed: the distance between them is closing, the cheetah is steadily gaining ground. But, abruptly, she runs out of steam and the sprint is over. None of us can speak, that's how mesmerised we are by what we've seen. Eventually, the cheetah's partner lopes slowly across to where the first one has abandoned the hunt. They sink down and the golden grasses close around them.

DAY 6
To Nossob Camp
Route
As we sip our early-morning coffee on the deck at Gharagab, we are surprised by the long, rasping groan of a lion in the distance. This is repeated twice, at long intervals. The urge to get on the road and track our cat is strong. So we take leave of our favourite camp, whose postage-stamp-size trough[11] nevertheless has drawn gemsbok, hartebeest, springbok and jackal to its life-giving waters.

And, yes, the spoor of sizable paws draws us on an anticipatory trail down the sand road out of Gharagab.[18] Alas, the lion eludes us, his spoor eventually veering off into the grasses.

But that's what Kgalagadi is all about, I muse. It's the anticipation, the suspense, moments filled with such fleeting possibility. This is what

... the cheetah moves at a speed that's breathtaking

keeps us coming back for more … and more … that precise moment of timing that brings such reward.

And believe me, you can drive for an hour, two hours, without seeing any semblance of life. This is when you understand the infinite space of the Kalahari; we experience only a sliver of its great expanse. Patience is what's required, and that's where the heightening effects of anticipation come in.

Camp details
Once again Nossob is our stepping stone – this time on our way to Bitterpan, dead centre between the Auob and Nossob riverbeds.

Highlight
Don't discount this 'non-wilderness' camp! Early in the evening, after hearing a soft bubbling '*p-p-p-whoo*' outside our chalet, I discover a pair of Southern White-faced Scops-Owls nesting in a honey locust tree beside our kitchen! With distinct white face masks lined in black, they peer down at me through big bright orange eyes. I'm utterly thrilled.

Then, after dinner, we decide to give the water hole one last whirl before turning in. As we creak along the boardwalk to the hide, wildly gesticulating arms wave us inside … and there, lapping thirstily not 5m away, are two solidly built female lions, their wide-eyed gaze fixed piercingly on the hide. We are so focused on them, we don't at first notice the Verreaux's Eagle-Owl seated on a dead trunk within the spotlight's ambit. From out of a pale face it gives us an unblinking stare, then flies back and forth on huge wings following its invisible prey. The lions, sated, head straight for the hide – everyone inside scrambles to get a better view – and they pass beneath us, then turn with the fence, following it into darkness.

Our day is complete.

DAYS 7 AND 8
To Bitterpan Camp
Route
On hearing that cheetah had been spotted the previous day near Nossob, we decide to do Marie se Draai before heading out to Bitterpan. We aren't prepared for the line of vehicles that stake their claim in front of the gateway before opening time, but we all pass through pretty fast. It's a morning of little excitement … until we stop to investigate a tree stump in the distance, poking up through the grasses. Our binoculars tell a different story: there

are four young cheetah cubs being watched over by their mother. Watching her for a while, we see her limp badly (another injured cat!) to a fallen tree trunk, behind which she conceals herself while still maintaining a vigilant watch. She must have called to her cubs as, one by one, they trail towards her to play under her watchful eye. Moving forward, we spot with some relief the male stretched out under a tree. At least there's one able body to do the hunting …

The 4x4-only route to Bitterpan (54km) starts out from inside Nossob Camp. Again, we cross the hilly, grassed dune land that fills the ample space between the two dry riverbeds. The route – up-down, up-down – is a very narrow single track fringed by *driedoring* bushes and camel-thorns.

We drive into a Georgia O'Keeffe sky: a white puzzle of patty-pan clouds cemented in powder blue. At every rise we look down on lustrous feathered grasses that resemble rollers rippling across a boundless ocean. Only Northern Black Korhaans interrupt our journey with their shrill cackle. Two big-eared steenbokkies, positively quivering with curiosity, do a couple of mock-charges at our stationary vehicles before thinking the better of it.

Camp details

A communal kitchen and central *lapa*⑯ area separate two units to one side and two to the other. Constructed from corrugated iron,

… a supple cat-like creature leaps from a tree … it's a leopard …

wood, canvas and reeds, the entire complex is linked by a wooden walkway. On one side of the walkway is the sleeping unit – two beds, a shelf and a deck – and on the other, a toilet, basin and shower. The camp faces onto an enormous flat, dry pan cradled by grassed and vegetated dunes, and between camp and pan is a small pumped water hole.

Highlight

Bitterpan is known for its lion and leopard, but we've learned to ignore the breathless reports and take each day as it comes. The first night, not even the yowl of a jackal pierces our dreams. The following afternoon – the camp is full – someone sees a supple cat-like creature leap from a tree onto the road leading away from Bitterpan into the dunes. It's a leopard. And it's loping towards us. One couple, bristling with 'bush expert' status, loses not a second. Wielding camera lenses the size of satellite dishes, they leap into their 4x4 and, in their infinite wisdom, tear up the road to photograph the elusive creature. I needn't elaborate on what happens next.

And so begins a very long afternoon of cat outsitting vehicle. From its hideout in the yellow grasses, the leopard keeps a watchful eye on the road, sitting up, then down, and up again. The vehicle starts its engine and creeps forward, and down goes the leopard. Back at camp we watch, speechless at the mind-numbingly selfish behaviour of our so-called wildlife experts. They're spoiling our own experience of a close encounter, and their 4x4 is blocking the cat's path to the water hole. Two tense gemsbok and a yipping black-backed jackal keep vigil at the pan. By the time the sun sinks behind the dunes (and the light is fast waning), the cat's patience wears thin. It does a long slow detour ahead of the 4x4, whose engine, I kid you not, fires into life, startling the leopard into a backtrack to its hideout.

The couple might have been subjected to a long night of slow torture – had their fingernails pulled, maybe? – had the leopard not decided to follow the road to our units anyway. It pads silently around the ranger's unit, then slinks *right in front* of our deck, crouching a metre from us and fixing us with a flinty green-eyed stare. None of us is breathing. Suddenly it bounds off, back to the ranger's hut to a tiny pool of water, where (finally!) it slakes its thirst. Then it's enfolded by the dusk.

DAY 9
Urikaruus Wilderness Camp
Route
The one-way return track to the Auob is similar to the route in, but the sand is softer, the *middelmannetjie* grassier and the inclines and descents steeper. Today, the air is cold and brittle – a frigid 2°C – but the grasses are lustrous in the honeyed morning light.⑫

It appears that it's too cold for anything to stir; hard as we peer out, we see nothing bar a duiker, a curious steenbok peeping at us from behind a bush and lots of dun-coloured larks difficult to identify. Grasses become dense with *driedoring*. Then camel-thorn, grey camel-thorn and twisted shepherd's trees dominate.

Spotted – raptors
Cape Vulture
White-backed Vulture
Tawny Eagle
Bateleur⑬ (junior)
Wahlberg's Eagle
Martial Eagle
Black-chested Snake-Eagle
Steppe Eagle
Steppe Buzzard
Lanner Falcon
Pygmy Falcon
Red-necked Falcon
Montagu's Harrier
Pale Chanting Goshawk
Gabar Goshawk

Spotted – ground birds
Ostrich
Kori Bustard⑭
Secretary Bird
Burchell's Sandgrouse
Northern Black Korhaan
Crowned Lapwing (Plover)

Spotted – pretty birds
Brown-crowned Tchagra
Groundscraper Thrush
Crimson-breasted Shrike
Yellow Canary
Bokmakierie
Lilac-breasted Roller⑮
Swallow-tailed Bee-eater
Kalahari Scrub Robin
Namaqua Dove
Ant-eating Chat
Red-headed Finch
Red-billed Quelea
Black-chested Prinia

Back on the dry Auob riverbed, the activity is all in the sky. Eleven vultures circle lazily above us, gliding, spiralling, far more elegant in the air than sitting in ungainly fashion on their treetop nests. Open-mouthed, we watch the aerial acrobatics of a scarlet-legged Bateleur confronting a vulture. Twice, its talons shoot out to give the vulture a healthy *skop* in mid-air.

We're also amazed at how prolific the flaming cerise flashes of Crimson-breasted Shrikes are; we'd read that they're highly secretive birds. Not here, not right now.

Camp details
Urikaruus (meaning 'white calcrete' – obviously a resource of abundance in the area) stole our hearts; we came pretty close to giving it instant 'favourite camp' status.

The four split-level units are of wood-frame and moulded prefabricated panels, topped by barrel roofs, and are linked by a wooden walkway. The units are painted green and lined with reeds. The second-level bedroom/shower is offset from the kitchen/dining area by a set of stairs adjacent to, rather than above, the first level. A deck off the kitchen overlooks a water hole (floodlit at night – yay!) in the Auob riverbed. Grazing quietly below us are a solitary wildebeest, gemsbok and a trio of springbok.

Highlight
At dusk it's the tense alertness of the springbok – frozen stares, whistling, snorting – that catches our attention. A spotlight from the next-door unit leaps and dances in the darkness, and there it is: a leopard, beautifully illuminated in the beam, has crept in behind us to investigate our camp. Totally unperturbed by the light picking it out and our hushed breathlessness as we tiptoe creakingly along the boardwalk to follow the leopard's path, it sniffs around the cars, then explores the space beneath our units. At times it's less than a metre away. We're spellbound by its presence, this exquisite creature usually so elusive and secretive … and here we've been honoured to witness it *twice*. It merges with the night as it makes its way to the water hole.

> **We're spellbound by its presence …**

Later on, we spot a caracal with its devilish pointed ears lapping at the water, and watch the weird kangaroo-like jumps of two springhares foraging in the grasses within the spotlight's pool of light. The screech of a Barn Owl and the *'hoo!'* of a Spotted Eagle-Owl clinch it for us on our last night in the Kgalagadi wilderness. It's been an unforgettable visit.

DAY 10
Twee Rivieren Camp/Exit
Travellers have the option to stay at Twee Rivieren at the park entrance – a camp of pretty pebble-walled units with low-hanging thatch and splayed support poles – before heading back home. But here, be warned, you seriously leave the wilderness behind … you're back to ceaseless activity, sounds of traffic at night and barking dogs. It's perhaps better to head directly down to Upington, making your home-straight plans from there.

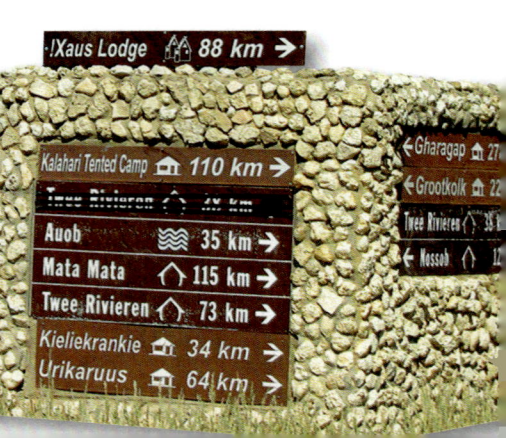

Melton Wold Guest House

If you're into an 'olde Englishe worlde' of heavy drapes, chandeliers, animal trophy heads and Oregon pine floors so polished you can see your reflection, this guest farm and hunting lodge, 40km outside Victoria West, might interest you on your way home. Parts of the main farmhouse date to 1889: its walls carry posters of old Dutch and British masters, and the Deer and Pheasant pub features Tudor-style timber panelling, stuffed pheasants and a glowing fireplace. The enormous sprawling lodge has 23 rooms (containing old-fashioned transistor radios that still work) interspersed with sitting rooms, parlours and games rooms. Following the 1930s Depression, Melton Wold's wealthy British landowner at the time invited destitute friends to share his home. Thereafter, its guesthouse status stuck. The name is a combination of the Melton stud farm in Australia, from where the original owner imported his horses, and the Cotswolds from where the owner's family originated. Don't expect haute cuisine, though: it's very plain, old-fashioned British fare.
Visit: www.meltonwold.co.za

Odd man out

You may have noticed that Grootkolk Wilderness Camp hasn't had a mention. The reason is, simply, that it was fully booked when we made our reservations. We did, however, check it out and take pictures. Set in among the dunes and overlooking a water hole, the four units resemble the sandbag-and-canvas design flair of Kalahari Tented Camp (and, like Kalahari, they have a ceiling fan). Each unit's kitchen is on the verandah and there is also a communal kitchen.

PLAN YOUR TRIP!

♦ **Web resources:**
www.sanparks.org/parks/kgalagadi;
www.peaceparks.org;
www.murrayguestfarm.co.za;
www.meltonwold.co.za

♦ Extra tourist resources and contacts: *see* pages 158–160

OUR EXPERIENCE

♦ **Best move on the trip:**
Booking into one of the camps for two nights (Bitterpan was our choice). Since the animals roam across such vast distances, you're not always guaranteed wildlife sightings: one night we didn't see or hear a peep, the next we were one-on-one with a leopard.

♦ **Worst move:**
Choose your neighbours if you can! Certain camps, like Bitterpan, with its communal kitchen and lapa, are a better experience when enjoyed with friends. Certain individuals (the ones you don't choose) can be unbelievably self-centred and it's best to avoid sharing space with them.

♦ **Our advice to you:**
Three wilderness camps – Urikaruus, Kieliekrankie and Gharagab – were closely tied for absolute favourite camp in Kgalagadi. People's tastes differ though … so choose one (or more) of the above – you can't go wrong! – and treat yourself to an extra day there.

Back-roads Kruger

Round trip 48km starting/ending Satara Camp

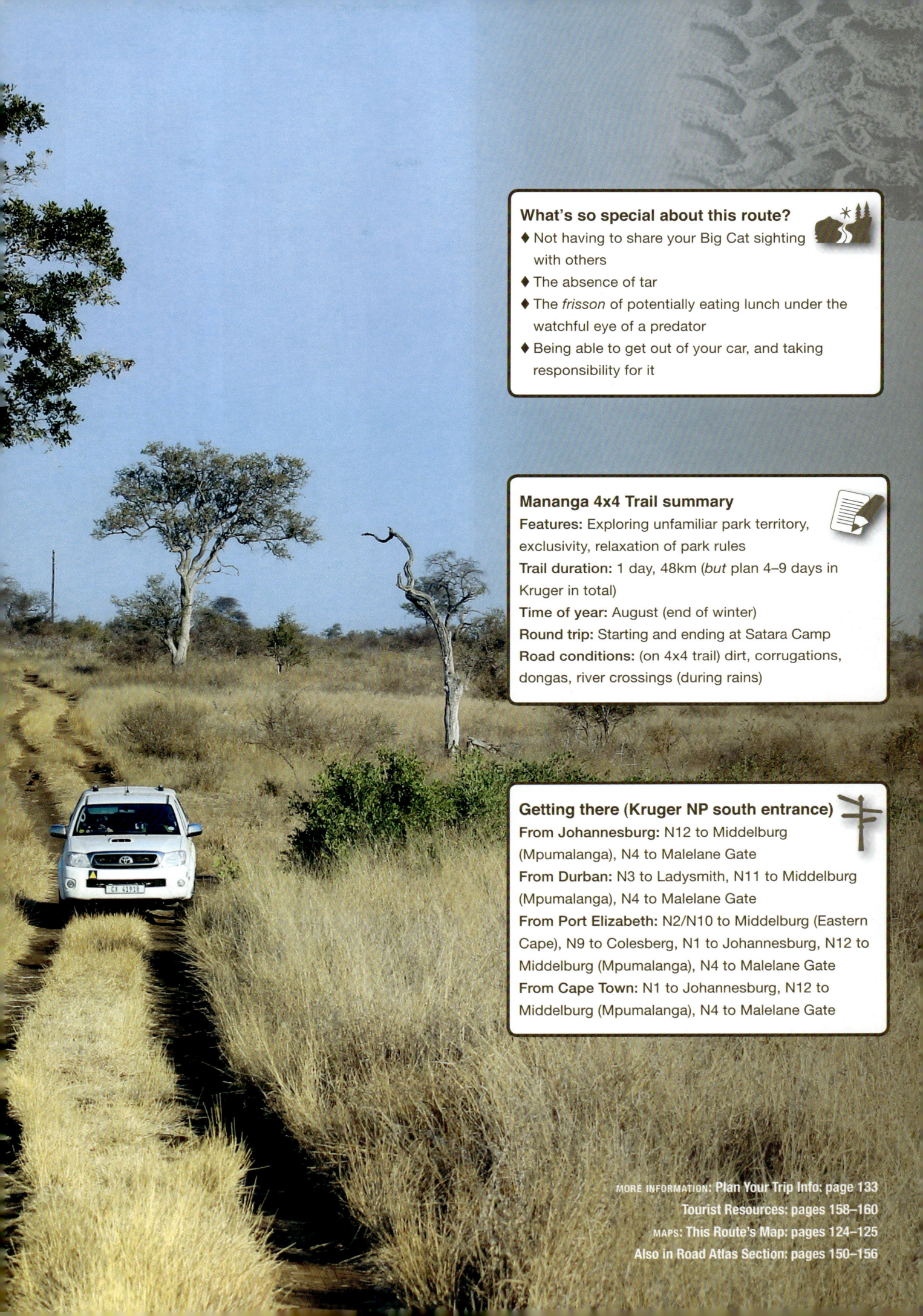

What's so special about this route?
♦ Not having to share your Big Cat sighting with others
♦ The absence of tar
♦ The *frisson* of potentially eating lunch under the watchful eye of a predator
♦ Being able to get out of your car, and taking responsibility for it

Mananga 4x4 Trail summary
Features: Exploring unfamiliar park territory, exclusivity, relaxation of park rules
Trail duration: 1 day, 48km (*but* plan 4–9 days in Kruger in total)
Time of year: August (end of winter)
Round trip: Starting and ending at Satara Camp
Road conditions: (on 4x4 trail) dirt, corrugations, dongas, river crossings (during rains)

Getting there (Kruger NP south entrance)
From Johannesburg: N12 to Middelburg (Mpumalanga), N4 to Malelane Gate
From Durban: N3 to Ladysmith, N11 to Middelburg (Mpumalanga), N4 to Malelane Gate
From Port Elizabeth: N2/N10 to Middelburg (Eastern Cape), N9 to Colesberg, N1 to Johannesburg, N12 to Middelburg (Mpumalanga), N4 to Malelane Gate
From Cape Town: N1 to Johannesburg, N12 to Middelburg (Mpumalanga), N4 to Malelane Gate

MORE INFORMATION: **Plan Your Trip Info: page 133**
Tourist Resources: pages 158–160
MAPS: **This Route's Map: pages 124–125**
Also in Road Atlas Section: pages 150–156

Back-roads Kruger

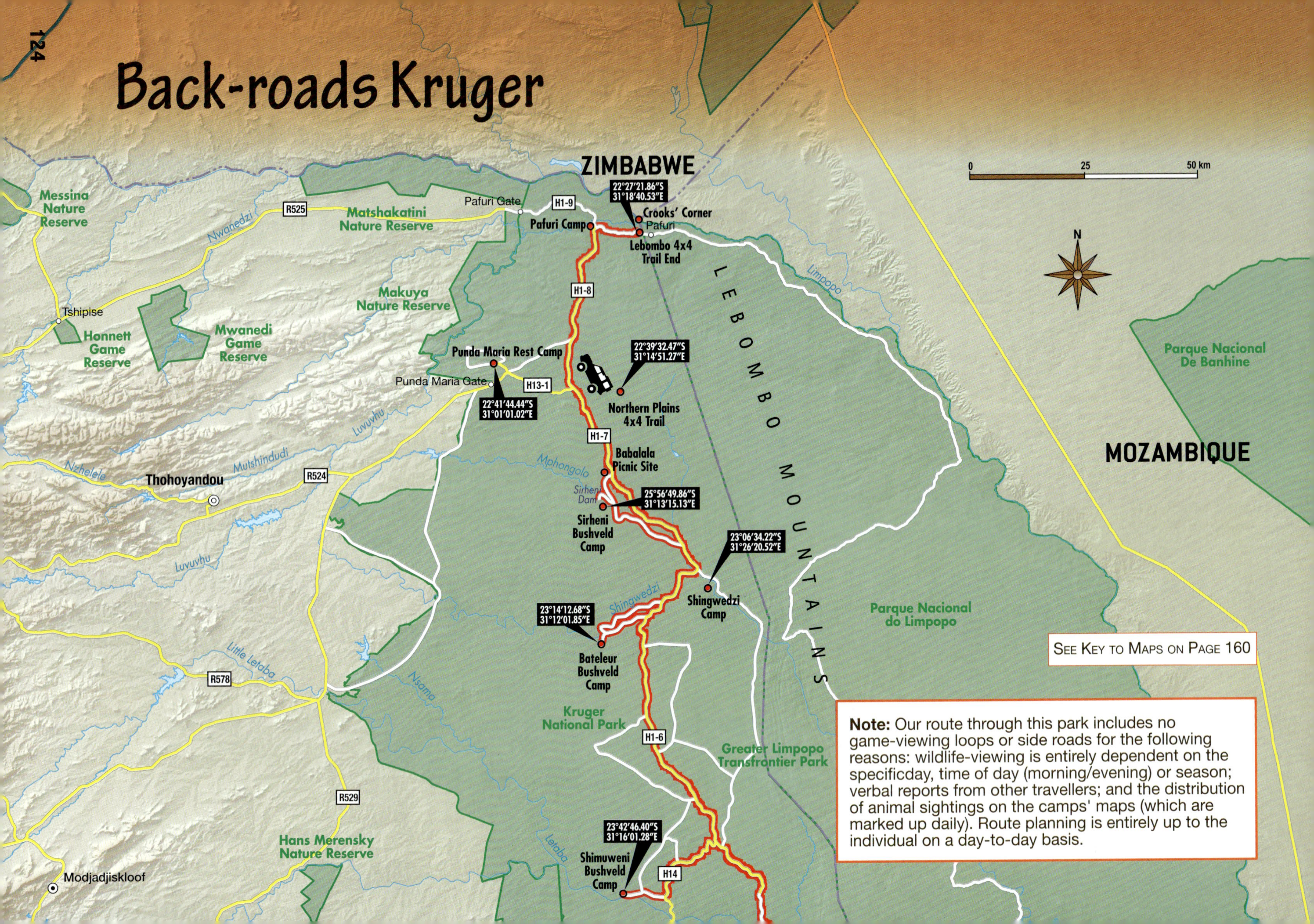

ZIMBABWE
MOZAMBIQUE
LEBOMBO MOUNTAINS
0 25 50 km
N
Messina Nature Reserve
Matshakatini Nature Reserve
Makuya Nature Reserve
Honnett Game Reserve
Mwanedi Game Reserve
Hans Merensky Nature Reserve
Kruger National Park
Greater Limpopo Transfrontier Park
Parque Nacional do Limpopo
Parque Nacional De Banhine
Tshipise
Thohoyandou
Modjadjiskloof
Pafuri Gate
Pafuri Camp
Pafuri
Crooks' Corner
22°27'21.86"S 31°18'40.53"E
Lebombo 4x4 Trail End
Punda Maria Rest Camp
Punda Maria Gate
22°41'44.44"S 31°01'01.02"E
Northern Plains 4x4 Trail
22°39'32.47"S 31°14'51.27"E
Babalala Picnic Site
Sirheni Dam
Sirheni Bushveld Camp
25°56'49.86"S 31°13'15.13"E
Shingwedzi Camp
23°06'34.22"S 31°26'20.52"E
Bateleur Bushveld Camp
23°14'12.68"S 31°12'01.85"E
Shimuweni Bushveld Camp
23°42'46.40"S 31°16'01.28"E
H1-9
H1-8
H1-7
H1-6
H13-1
H14
R525
R524
R578
R529
Limpopo
Nwanedzi
Luvuvhu
Mutshindudi
Nzhelele
Mphongolo
Shingwedzi
Little Letaba
Nsama
Letaba

See Key to Maps on Page 160

Note: Our route through this park includes no game-viewing loops or side roads for the following reasons: wildlife-viewing is entirely dependent on the specificday, time of day (morning/evening) or season; verbal reports from other travellers; and the distribution of animal sightings on the camps' maps (which are marked up daily). Route planning is entirely up to the individual on a day-to-day basis.

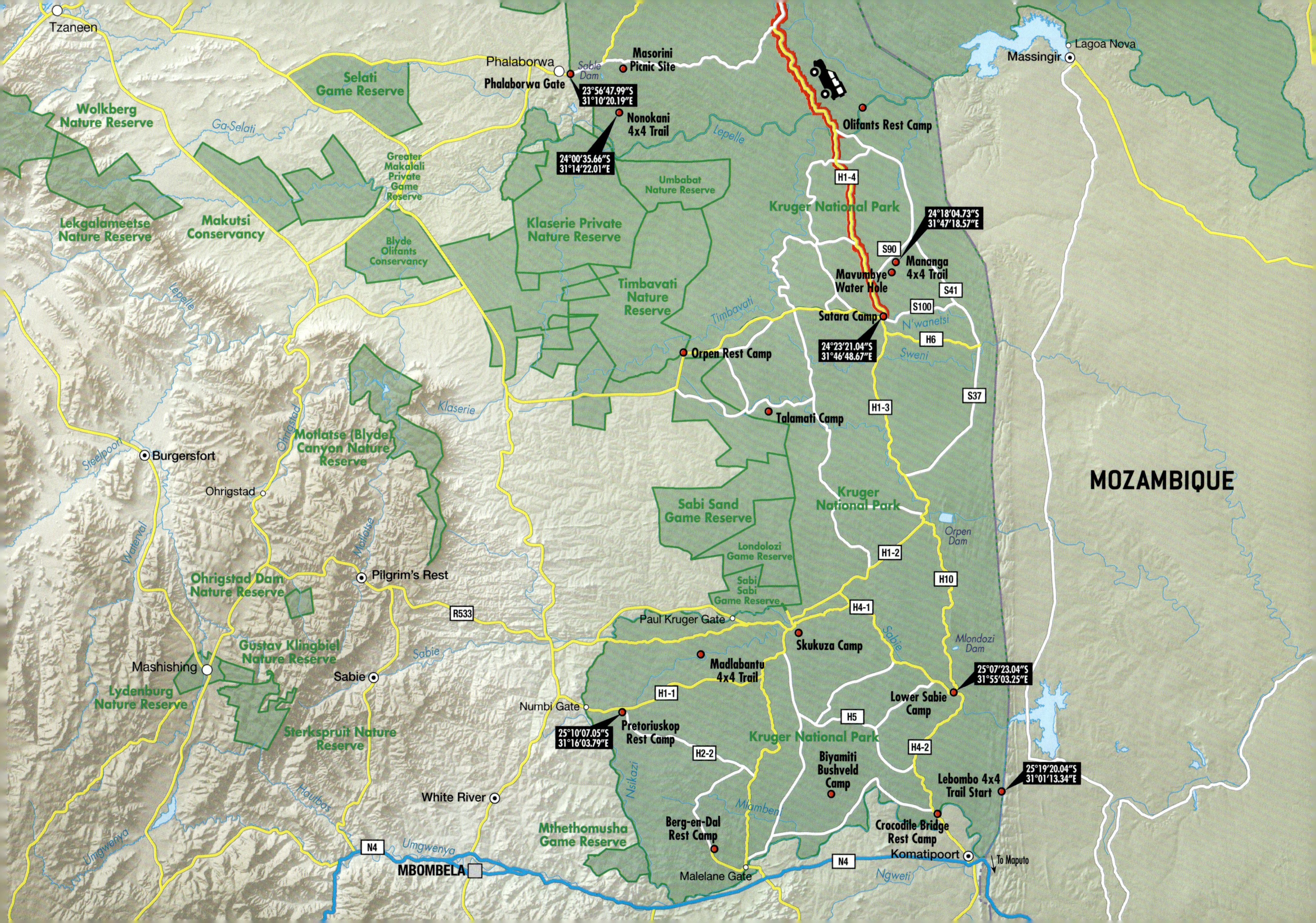
MOZAMBIQUE
Kruger National Park
Kruger National Park
Kruger National Park
Tzaneen
Phalaborwa
Phalaborwa Gate
23°56'47.99"S 31°10'20.19"E
Sable Dam
Masorini Picnic Site
Nonokani 4x4 Trail
24°00'35.66"S 31°14'22.01"E
Olifants Rest Camp
Lagoa Nova
Massingir
Selati Game Reserve
Wolkberg Nature Reserve
Ga-Selati
Greater Makalali Private Game Reserve
Lepelle
Umbabat Nature Reserve
Klaserie Private Nature Reserve
Lekgalameetse Nature Reserve
Makutsi Conservancy
Blyde Olifants Conservancy
Timbavati Nature Reserve
H1-4
24°18'04.73"S 31°47'18.57"E
S90
Mananga 4x4 Trail
Mavumbye Water Hole
S41
S100
Timbavati
Satara Camp
N'wanetsi
24°23'21.04"S 31°46'48.67"E
H6
Sweni
Orpen Rest Camp
S37
Klaserie
Talamati Camp
H1-3
Steelpoort
Burgersfort
Ohrigstad
Motlatse (Blyde) Canyon Nature Reserve
Ohrigstad
Sabi Sand Game Reserve
Londolozi Game Reserve
Sabi Sabi Game Reserve
Orpen Dam
Waterval
Motlatse
H1-2
H10
Pilgrim's Rest
Ohrigstad Dam Nature Reserve
R533
Paul Kruger Gate
H4-1
Skukuza Camp
Sabie
Mlondozi Dam
Gustav Klingbiel Nature Reserve
Mashishing
Sabie
Sabie
Madlabantu 4x4 Trail
25°07'23.04"S 31°55'03.25"E
Lydenburg Nature Reserve
H1-1
Lower Sabie Camp
Numbi Gate
H5
Pretoriuskop Rest Camp
25°10'07.05"S 31°16'03.79"E
Sterkspruit Nature Reserve
H2-2
H4-2
Biyamiti Bushveld Camp
Lebombo 4x4 Trail Start
25°19'20.04"S 31°01'13.34"E
Nsikazi
Houtbos
White River
Mlambeni
Berg-en-Dal Rest Camp
Mthethomusha Game Reserve
Crocodile Bridge Rest Camp
Umgwenya
N4
Umgwenya
MBOMBELA
Malelane Gate
N4
Ngweti
Komatipoort
To Maputo

Kruger's 4x4 self-drive trails
Starting from:
- *Shingwedzi* – **Northern Plains** (49km): Starting at Babalala picnic site, it promises remoteness and solitude; mopane, leadwood and sickle bush; baobabs in the sandveld; good bird-watching.
- *Phalaborwa Gate* – **Nonokani**, meaning 'drive slowly' (46km): Starting at Masorini picnic site, it promises mopane, red and russet bushwillow woodland on the way to Reenvoël Dam; riverine forest along the Lepelle River; mopane on the leg to Sable Dam; elephant, antelope and, possibly, lion.
- *Satara* – **Mananga**, meaning 'wilderness' (48km): It promises open-tree savannah of knob-thorn acacia, leadwood, marula and round-leaved teak; grazing antelope; potential for Big Five and cheetah.
- *Pretoriuskop* – **Madlabantu**, meaning 'man-eater' (42km): It promises cluster-leaf and bushwillow, round-leaved and wild teak woodland; possibly Big Five and rhino around the Nsikazi River.

What's the appeal?
- Remoteness (only six vehicles permitted per day); unfamiliar terrain (normally closed to public); a different bush experience – you may get out of your vehicle *prudently* and *at own risk*.
- Trails are *not* technically difficult, bar a few dongas and river crossings (trails closed in wet season).
- Reservation is permitted only at the relevant camp, on the morning of the trail; cost R470* per vehicle plus R100 deposit to be reclaimed on return (in case of the need for rescue).

* Note: monetary values given here were current at the end of 2012.

Kruger's guided trail
The five-day **Lebombo Trail** (up to eight vehicles, accompanied by an armed guide/ranger) tracks Kruger's eastern border from Komatipoort to Pafuri. There are no facilities and all 4x4s must be entirely self-sufficient.

Okay, guys, we know, we know: Kruger is not 4x4 territory. But what is an off-road book on Southern Africa if it doesn't make even the briefest mention of a wilderness tract that's the size of Wales? Our plan was to experience one of Kruger's 4x4 trails, test out some of the bush camps and, once we'd made the long trek there – it's a long drive from Knysna – explore the park from north to south via the untarred back roads as much as possible.

TRAIL DAY
Satara Camp: Mananga 4x4 Trail (48km)
Leg time (including coffee and lunch stops): 5½ hours

The reservations office opened at 07:00, but Hirsh was at the door *way* earlier. Our hearts were set on the trail – this book depended on it – and we were dumbstruck at the tally of foreign visitors trawling Kruger in hired 4x4s and abused sedans. A trail limit of six vehicles per day was dramatically undermining our chances … we were not going to be outsmarted by *uitlanders*.

So Hirsh was the first to slap his money down. Kruger's off-road trails don't profess to challenge diehard 4x4-ers; the point is to have a different bushveld experience without being tailed by 10 cars, with the freedom to step out of your vehicle (wisely), and the option to wander all day, if you so wish, on roads that are out of bounds to high traffic.

Dues paid, deposit exacted, permit and trail map in hand, the Freelander and Hilux were through Satara's gates at 07:30. The spidery arms of the Mananga Trail, in the lower half of Kruger, are contained within the triangle of the S90, S41 and S100 – the latter road one of the park's most loved, tried and tested. It files along the N'wanetsi River through huge river-hugging trees and tree-savannah grasslands, a perfect habitat for antelope③ and large purring (and coughing) felines.

We started through yellow-straw grassland, interspersed with spiky denuded trees: knob-thorn acacia, marula, teak and bushwillow (the last the only species recognisable by its winged-pod clusters). A hopeful sign was the fresh patty-pan tracks of an elephant in the chocolate soil. Later we spotted him some distance away – too far to get excited. The road, with a high-grass *middelmannetjie*, turned hard and pitted. Large round boulders embedded in the earth made a half-hearted attempt at giving us 4x4 terrain. Keith's eagle eyes spotted a rhino, mine caught a glimpse of a foraging honey badger.

Stately-horned male kudu gave us wide-eyed stares; the oversized ears of female kudus quivered with alertness; zebra with adorable foals threw us quizzical glances … but there were also long stretches where not a whisker twitched.

Patience is key. Anyone who's been to Kruger knows that you have to work *really* hard to tick off all the animals on your wish list. In winter visibility is good – the trees are scratchy and leafless – but most water holes are sun-baked earth and every wise creature is hanging out in a damp riverbed. So unless you're near one, don't count on seeing too much.

At a water hole on the Mavumbye stream, a sizable collection of vultures – some planing in on massive wingspans, others doing a running takeoff, the rest simply basking in the warmth, giant feathers splayed – had us gawking for a while through our binoculars. Three species were gathered here, all in one melting pot: Hooded, Cape and White-backed.

Where the trail connects up with the N'wanetsi River, we had time to marvel at the enormous canopied, and quite beautiful, riverine trees: grey-crackle trunks of tall jackal-berry, yellow-cream buttresses of giant

… zebra with adorable foals threw us quizzical glances …

127

sycamore figs, densely branched weeping boer-bean and the bulbous knotted girths of gargantuan nyalas.

A troop of ginger-maned giraffes with surprisingly dark-dappled coats nibbled delicately.④ A couple of fallen trees, flattened by the might of elephants, barricaded the road but a detour had already been beaten out by tyre tracks. Some steep descents into the riverbed had us contemplating how hellish this drive could become during the rains. It was 11:30, there was plenty of rhino dung around, but by now nothing stirred. This went on for so long, I feared our off-road adventure was doomed to end up benign and tame.

Excitement ratcheted up a notch when we rounded a corner and right there, beside us, was an enormous bull elephant with upcurved tusks. He was pretty nonplussed, so we edged quietly past him.⑨ A loop of the trail had taken us back to the Mavumbye water hole, where a rabble of White-backed Vultures still lingered, but it was the tension in the necks of three nearby giraffes that caught our eye. Keith spotted the instigators. Two young male lions,⑦ having just skirted the water hole, loped languidly through the waist-high grasses. Our vehicles crept closer; the lions paused and turned their faces toward us, then dissolved into the wheaten bushveld.

Spotted
Woolly-necked Stork
Saddle-billed Stork
Goliath Heron
White-crowned Lapwing
Grey-headed Parrot
Southern Yellow-billed Hornbill⑤
Red-billed Hornbill
Crowned Hornbill
Grey Go-away-bird
Burchell's Coucal
Lilac-breasted Roller
Arrow-marked Babbler
White-browed Robin-Chat
Pin-tailed Whydah
Crested Barbet
Black-collared Barbet
Magpie Shrike
White-crested Helmet Shrike
Gorgeous Bush-Shrike
Burchell's and Meves's Starling
Green Wood-Hoopoe
White-fronted Bee-eater⑥
White-bellied Sunbird

It was midday – so much for the constant refrain that you have to be up early to catch the Big Cats. Luckily for us, the trail road crossed the dry riverbed and headed in their general direction. We progressed slowly, eyes peeled for movement – an ear twitching, a dark mane against the yellow grasses. And there, under a skeletal tree, sat *three* young males in a tight huddle, fitting together like puzzle pieces, manes all lined up. We switched off our engines; they were fully aware of us. One sat up, throwing a fierce glare from honeyed eyes in our direction. He glowered a while, lowering his head briefly for a better look at us, then slowly, deliberately, moved to another tree and flopped down. Exhilarated, we watched the lions for an age, revelling in our private viewing experience. No rumbling engines, no vehicles jostling for supremacy. We sat undisturbed, the rustling of the bushveld the only sound in the still air. After the cats had clearly settled in for a snooze, we reluctantly moved on.

> **I feared our off-road adventure was doomed to end up benign and tame**

An animated lunch was enjoyed under a shady leadwood (after careful inspections for creatures crouching in the underbrush). As we wended our way slowly back, Keith spotted a herd of wildebeest that, on closer inspection, turned out to be buffalo.

So, in the end, benign the 4x4 trail certainly didn't prove to be. Effectively we'd seen four of the Big Five. Now, that was something to write about.

Kruger, the great debate: north versus south?

The north

There is no doubt that the remoteness of the north engenders a more exclusive experience – it is wilder, less trafficked, with more bush camps. You get to see tracts of fat baobabs with their Medusa heads and shiny trunks gored and torn and stripped by elephants' tusks. (They do this to get to the nutrients beneath the bark.) There are also luminous groves of fever trees the colour of yellowed parchment. Along the watercourses you stare in wonder at gargantuan, knobbly, magical trees just like Ents out of *Lord of the Rings*.

And there's a chance of seeing the more unusual animals – we spied Sharpe's grysbok, suni antelope, Lichtenstein's hartebeest and my special favourite, sable antelope. (No wild dog, though.) Although the cats are more prolific in the open savannah of the south, we had a brief encounter one morning with a big male lion resting at the roadside. And late one evening, at Sirheni Bush Camp, Hirsh and I listened enthralled as two males conversed across the bushveld: a long, drawn-out, hoarse groan, building up to a series of shuddering grunts, getting closer and closer each time.

In both halves of Kruger you work hard, though, at your wildlife viewing. We were visiting at the end of a long, dry winter; only the mopanes bore a mantle of russet, caramel and sour-green. And yet, the camouflage offered by brittle twigs and branches and clouds of nests was ingenious. We watched kudu and waterbuck – in fact, entire herds of elephant and buffalo – dematerialise in skeletal brush flanking the road. One minute they had substance, the next you'd never have known they existed. We can't imagine how difficult it must be to spot a grey rump or the switch of a tail in the robust, leafy, closed vegetation of summer. But then again, it's all about luck: being in the right place at the right time. You want to be there at the precise moment an animal steps out onto the road.

In both north and south, and always at rivers and water holes, we encountered plenty of elephant,

129

some with the teeniest babies, dinky enough to slip beneath the girth of their mothers' stomachs. We met up with enormous herds – up to 80 or 90 individuals – of buffalo giving us somnambulant stares, their short-horned littlies just like domestic calves. And in every river, the round buffed and polished rocks were, in fact, pod after pod of hippo throwing us baleful looks,⑧ then sighing and slowly submerging, leaving only a trail of bubbles on the surface of the water. Crocodiles, too, were on early summer camp; rock shelves and sandbanks were encrusted with spines, scales, claws and razor teeth, as they soporifically absorbed the sun's rays, fearsome jaws agape.

The south
I'm afraid my prejudices towards southern Kruger's tar, traffic congestion and car pile-ups at any sighting of significance were pulverised on this trip. It was ridiculous – we got up close with all of the Big Five *and* cheetah … in *one day*. You just can't argue with that.

On a morning that began at Satara Camp with the *'whooo-oo'* of spotted hyena,⑪ we took the popular S100 along the N'wanetsi River. For a long while nothing twitched, till we met an assembly line of cars. Perfectly poised on a rock in a riverbed flanking the road was a leopard. Rosette-dappled and gorgeous, fur backlit by the sun, it was sleepily aware of the consternation it was causing. We watched till it got up, languidly climbed down and padded off to a bush thicket, where it sank out of sight.

Our first white rhino, which up till now had been weirdly absent (blame it on those heinous poachers), was slumbering beneath an acacia, curved horn artfully picked out by the sun. A little later, two prehistoric grazing heads didn't pause once to come up for air. Both sightings were from a tar road.

As we travelled south to Lower Sabie Camp, we spotted buffalo, big-bossed and muddy, at Orpen Dam. Along the way the elephant – a herd of six bulls, one enormous, with a chopped tusk – raised our blood levels somewhat.⑩ Purposefully bearing down on us from the side – scary enough for us to swiftly close our windows and briefly consider gunning the engine and vamoosing – they suddenly changed course and passed in front of our Freelander. A lone bull stayed behind on the road ahead. He hesitated, turned to face us, then lifted his foot, trunk swaying. We held our breath. He

... the round buffed and polished rocks were, in fact, pod after pod of hippo

changed his mind and ambled to the roadside. Bullets of sweat on our brows. Again, both animal encounters were just off the tar.

Our highlight was the cheetah. We'd left the tarred H10 to visit Mlondozi Dam. Just before arriving at the picnic site, not far off the road, wrapped around an anthill was a tangle of big dots and little dots: a female and her three cubs, limbs entwined, soft fur bristling. She was half-heartedly watching a herd of wildebeest some distance away, sussing out her chances of an easy meal for her brood. At times she'd turn her painted face, with its amber eyes, freckles and dramatic black cheek-liner, to gaze beautifully at us. We couldn't tear our eyes away. We sat for over an hour, watching the young cubs stretch and yawn and inconsiderately trample all over momma.⑫

You'd think that was enough for one day. It was the end of an eventful afternoon; we were approaching the bridge that straddles the Sabie River to enter Lower Sabie Camp when a shaggy-maned lion crossed the road ahead of us! He padded into the brush, then, unbelievably, hesitated, turned and started back towards us. Now at the roadside, between our Freelander and a vehicle opposite, he paused to glare in our direction, then bounded between the two cars before disappearing.⑭

Five of the Big Five … check. We just couldn't be churlish about not seeing our wild dogs.

And, so, Kruger truly redeems itself. If you try hard enough, it's possible to find dirt (and I'd think during the rains the roads would become quite testing). There are gravel detours and off- road 4x4 trails, and although they're not technically challenging, this is more about soaking up the magic of the bush, listening to its secret language, easing into the pace of the natural world. It's a world driven by the presence of water or the lack thereof, the sun's trajectory across the sky,⑬ winter and spring, drought and rain. It's the tune of Africa.

Spotted (raptors)
White-backed Vulture
Cape Vulture
Hooded Vulture
Lappet-faced Vulture
Bateleur
African Crowned Eagle
Tawny Eagle
Brown Snake Eagle
African Fish Eagle⑮

Bush camps: our experience

What sets these camps apart is their exclusivity (sometimes there are only seven chalets); the access roads are limited to residents only (that means no day-trippers and no buses); and there are no shops or restaurants, so self-catering is key. This also spells peace and tranquillity.

Sirheni Bushveld Camp ①⑰
(Sirheni means 'cemetery' in Tsonga, named after a nearby elephant graveyard)

We stayed in a two-bedroom, two-bathroom guest cottage⑯ (single-room cottages are also available). The simple but very adequate units are set under mopanes and consist of thatch, tiled floors, an open lounge/kitchen, and a verandah with a table and chairs. They occupy a great position along the Mphongolo River with, to one side, Sirheni Dam. Hippos grunt below, the African Fish Eagle's cry is a constant refrain, and we heard lion calls in the night.

Bateleur Bushveld Camp
(Named after the scarlet-tailed eagle, dramatic to see in flight and plentiful in the park)

These small, two-bedroomed units,⑱ set in mopane woodland above the Mashokwe Spruit (it was a dry grassed valley in winter), constituted our least favourite of the bush camps (it had the least character). The kitchenette – fridge, sink, microwave, hotplate – and living area are housed under thatch on a tile-floor open verandah. There are no views to speak of, and the hide overlooking a water hole is outside the camp. (We were perplexed at SANParks' description of this particular camp as a 'luxury experience'. Perhaps it's the electricity, air conditioning and TV.)

Shimuweni Bushveld Camp
(Shimuweni means 'place of the baobab' in the Shangaan language; some enormous specimens line the Letaba River)

Now, *this* is what we call a luxury experience (although no electrical plug points). We stayed in a two-bedroom guest cottage,⑲ but simpler cottages are available. It has a stunning location, ranged on a ridge above the Letaba River, overlooking a large hippo pool. The units are modern, with lots of big sliding doors and windows, a kitchenette with a bar counter that faces a glassed verandah, an oversized outdoor table and chairs, and fans in the bedrooms. The camp comes with a resident tame Sharpe's grysbok. While we were there, a buffalo grazed on the opposite bank, a big family of elephant with littlies dined on grasses in the river, hippos and crocs hung out on the rocks. Definitely our favourite.

Note: there are two more bushveld camps in the south, Biyamiti and Talamati, which we didn't try.

PLAN YOUR TRIP!

♦ **Web resources:**
www.sanparks.co.za
http://sanparks.org.za/parks/kruger/tourism/activities/4x4_adv_trails.php
♦ Extra tourist resources and contacts: *see* pages 158–160

OUR EXPERIENCE

♦ **Best move on the trip:**
To explore Kruger's northern parts but also not to ignore the very busy south, despite the tar and 'high-season circus' perceptions. Our best animal sightings – and that includes the cat community – were in the south.

♦ **Worst move:**
Doubting Kruger's well-worn tar and much-maligned south!

♦ **Our advice to you:**
Kruger is the size of a small country, so it just can't be explored all in one trip. Choose one area and explore it thoroughly. Whizzing through in an effort to cover as much distance as possible doesn't work. We split northern and southern Kruger by visiting Mozambique in-between, which was a good move as there is only so much eye-peeling a person can do.

Southern-central Mozambique

Round trip
2120km
starting/ending
Giriyondo Border
Post (Kruger NP)

What's so special about this route?
- Cerulean sea; relatively unspoilt; shimmering, powder-fine sands
- Coconut palms, milkwoods and mangroves
- 4x4 sand driving
- Testing your 4x4's resilience to potholes and endlessly bad roads

Trip summary
Features: Soft-sand driving, beating the tide for beach drives, *really* bad road systems
Trip duration: 13 days, 2120km
Time of year: Beginning of August (end of winter)
Round trip: Starting and ending at Giriyondo Border Post (Kruger NP)
Road conditions: Badly potholed tar, loose-stone gravel, corrugations, mean speed humps, sand (beach driving **only with a permit**)

Getting there (Giriyondo/Kruger NP)
Note: Giriyondo is 91km from Phalaborwa Gate (allow 3 hours)
From Johannesburg: N1 to Polokwane, R71 to Phalaborwa (Kruger border)
From Durban: N3 to Ladysmith, N11 to Mokopane, N1 to Polokwane, R71 to Phalaborwa
From Port Elizabeth: N2/N10 to Middelburg, N9 to Colesberg, N1 to Polokwane, R71 to Phalaborwa
From Cape Town: N1 to Polokwane, R71 to Phalaborwa

MORE INFORMATION: **Plan Your Trip Info: page 149**
Tourist Resources: pages 158–160
MAPS: **This Route's Map: pages 136–137**
Also in Road Atlas Section: pages 150–156

Southern-central Mozambique

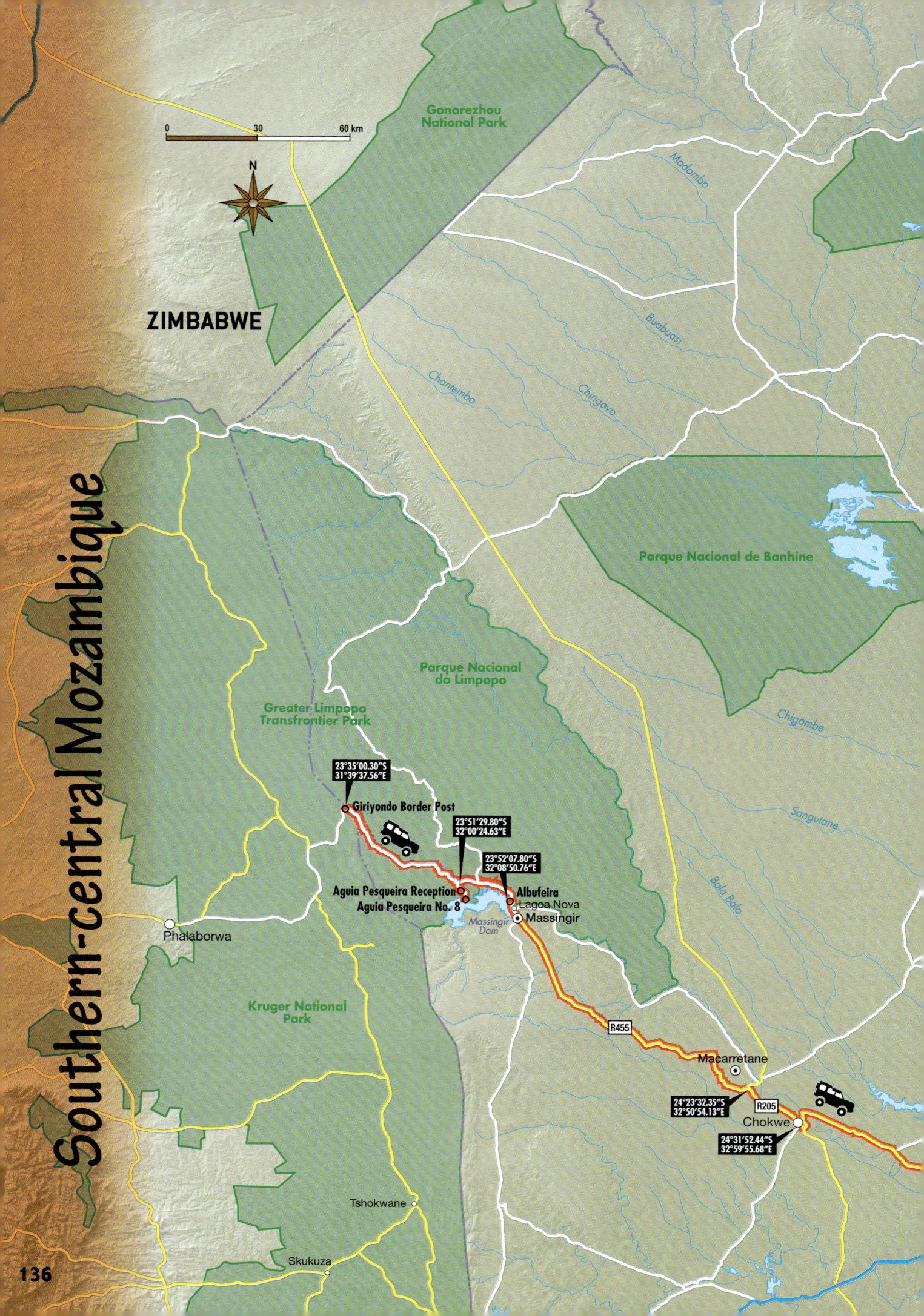

ZIMBABWE

Gonarezhou National Park

Parque Nacional de Banhine

Greater Limpopo Transfrontier Park

Parque Nacional do Limpopo

23°35'00.30"S
31°39'37.56"E
Giriyondo Border Post

23°51'29.80"S
32°00'24.63"E

23°52'07.80"S
32°08'50.76"E

Aguia Pesqueira Reception
Aguia Pesqueira No. 8

Albufeira
Lagoa Nova
Massingir

Massingir Dam

Phalaborwa

Kruger National Park

R455

Macarretane

R205

24°23'32.35"S
32°50'54.13"E

24°31'52.44"S
32°59'55.68"E

Chokwe

Tshokwane

Skukuza

136

B D Lodge; Johnson's Beach Bar
Beach Access (Permit)
21°30′17.04″S
35°11′09.72″E
EN1
Zombe
Inhassoro
21°32′05.40″S
35°12′03.54″E
21°33′53.13″S
35°05′56.78″E
Parque Nacional de Zinave
Chuambo
Vilanculos
21°59′30.98″S
35°14′23.18″E
Chinuane
Chichocane
Mapinhane
SEE KEY TO MAPS ON PAGE 160
Fornos
EN1
Nhachengue
Pomene
Pomene Lodge
MOZAMBIQUE
Unguana
Rio das Pedras
Massinga
Mocoduene
Morrumbene
23°50′41.60″S
35°30′04.40″E
Flamingo Bay Water Lodge
Praia do Tofo
Casa Barry
Macachula
Homoine
Inhambane
EN1
23°52′12.13″S
35°23′15.93″E
24°07′45.41″S
35°16′19.38″E
Panda
Cumbana
Paindane
Maqueze
Inhassume
Coguno
Inharrime
Chicomo
Ponta Zavora
INDIAN
OCEAN
Chibuto
EN1
Quissico
Zandamela
Malaira
25°01′10.86″S
33°47′46.98″E
Chidenguele
Sunset Beach Lodge
Xai-Xai

Mozambique: border formalities and requirements

- Minimum of one night's stay in either Kruger or Limpopo National Park is mandatory in order to use the Giriyondo Border Post.
- At the border, pay the national park fee of 200 meticais per person and another 200 meticais per vehicle (the metical/rand rate at the time of writing was 3:1)*; rands are accepted.
- At the border, pay the R10 importation fee per vehicle.
- Third-party motor insurance is required (R150); available in South Africa.
- Vehicle papers, consisting of car registration papers and a driver's licence.
- Two emergency triangles per vehicle (front and rear).
- Two reflector vests per vehicle (keep these visible while you drive).
- One fire extinguisher per vehicle (also keep visible).
- ZA sticker fixed to rear of vehicle.
- If towing anything (e.g. boat, trailer), purchase two stickers featuring a yellow triangle on a blue background; fix the small one on the front right bumper, the large one on the rear of whatever you're towing.
- If you're carrying passengers, they *must* buckle their seat belts.
- If you visit a Bureau de Change to buy meticais before crossing the border, you need your passport and proof of residence.
- Have some meticais (also in small denominations) to hand when crossing the border, as getting change for your rands, euros or dollars isn't going to happen.
- Your liquor allowances per vehicle are: 2 x 24 trays beer; 5 x 750ml bottles wine; 3 x 750ml bottles spirits.
- General speed limit is 60kph or 50kph in villages and built-up areas and 100kph on the open road. *Do not exceed these limits; you **will** be fined!*
- *Always* be courteous, polite and patient – this will get you a long, long way.
- *Never* ever give in to a bribe; rather ask where the closest police station is and suggest that you pay your fine there.

* Note: all monetary values given here were current at the end of 2012.

In terms of logistics, our trip to Mozambique was an add-on to our exploration of northern Kruger, but for practical purposes we've treated it as a separate chapter. And in light of the dire stories about Mozambique on 4x4 forums, in web reports and from travellers (arbitrary fines, vehicle searches, bribery, corruption), we took a conscious decision to avoid Maputo and the over-visited far southern parts. Instead, we used a quiet, little-used border post (excellent move!) and, on reaching the coast, drove northward.

DAY 1
Giriyondo Border Post to Massingir Dam (70km)
Time it took us: 2 hours

Border boot camp

It was a beautiful hot, clear African day – 30°C. As we approached Giriyondo through rock-strewn hills, the last 10km to the border served up stony gravel, embedded rock and corrugations. At the border, with just a little trepidation, we faced a posse of uniformed officials inside the immigration building as we handed over passports, vehicle papers and filled-out forms. They were all very polite and agreeable. Then came the vehicle inspections,① executed by a second posse. First vests, extinguishers and stickers were checked; next came the questions of what (and how much) we were carrying. Some of our plastic food-storage boxes were opened, but they were more interested in our beer quotient. It was within requirements. One immigration official, after not finding anything he could fine us for, was content to leave us alone.

Thinking we'd successfully run *that* gauntlet, we prepared to close up and move on. But the next customs official, who'd been hanging in the wings, sauntered over to do his own inspection. Another round of questions: Were we carrying any medicines? Hirsh, irrevocably honest, mentioned chronic medication. This, naturally, required inspection. 'Receipts,' the guy said. My heart sank to my flip-flops. And yet ... Hirsh still manages to surprise me. After a panicked instant, a desperate scrabble in the Freelander produced a Clicks packet, receipt neatly stowed inside. Scrutinising it for an interminably long moment, the official handed it back, satisfied. The ordeal was over.

We hotfooted it out of there as fast as Mozambique's speed limit would allow.

The drive
Our leg to Massingir Dam took us through the Limpopo National Park, part of the future Greater Limpopo Transfrontier Park, an initiative between South Africa, Mozambique and Zimbabwe to eventually remove the fences that separate the countries between the Kruger, Limpopo

> *The corrugated road was dusty, rutted and littered with loose stones ...*

and Gonarezhou parks. This move intends to open up ancient migratory routes used by elephant, and to encourage the transmigration of other wild animals between the countries.

However, the Mozambican park brochure handed to us at the border didn't inspire too much confidence in our chances of spying any wildlife. Words like 'undeveloped' and 'in the early stages' foretold of our fleeting glimpses of a solitary impala here and there – although the road was lined with plenty of dried elephant dung. The contrast in vegetation between the Kruger and Mozambican sides was so marked it was as if a line had been drawn in the sand: we were now in drab, leafless mopane veld so dry you could hear the last remnant leaves rattle. This evolved into stunted mopane on brick-red sands, then greener, tighter woodland. An African Grey Hornbill and a couple of Go-away-birds and Lilac-breasted Rollers enlivened the scene.

The corrugated road was dusty, rutted and littered with loose stones (the same brochure emphasised that the park's roads demanded a 4x4 vehicle). When we got to Campismo Albufeira at Massingir Dam, the short leg to our log cabins was humped and badly washed away② – definitely 4x4 territory.

Mode of abode
Holding our breath at what might await us, we were quite won over by the dinky A-frame reed-roofed log cabins③ with views through scrub to the massive Massingir Dam. Each unit contained two beds, a small table and two chairs, a kitchenette (with the barest of essentials) and fridge, and a toilet/basin with a thin-trickle shower. They were clean, there were mosquito nets and fans (ours didn't work at first, but an obliging camp official dealt with it), and bird song tittered and trilled around us. It was 34°C (at the tail end of winter), but we were comfortable and happy.

After the day's heat, we were surprised at sundown by a gusting wind that persisted into the night – not conducive to using the camp's braai discs raised on poles, which were perplexingly placed at the edge of the clearing, a burning ember's breath away from tinder-dry brush. Without an alternative dinner plan it made for an interesting evening. But we got away without setting the camp alight.

DAY 2
Massingir Dam to Casa Barry, Tofo (515km)
Time it took us: Massingir Dam to Chidenguele – 5 hours; Chidenguele to Tofo – 3½ hours

⇱ Take R455 southeast to Chokwe, at T-junction turn right onto R205 (Chokwe), left to Guija/Chongoene, left onto EN1 (Chidenguele), north up coastline (Quissico, Inharrime), right onto EN101 to Inhambane; leave Inhambane on EN259, right onto EN242 to Tofo

The drive
We crossed Massingir via a gigantic dam wall, where water streamed over concrete into the Maduxe River (the Lepelle flows into the dam to the west). The dam marked the end of the Limpopo NP for us. We were surrounded by very dry woodland of mopane, acacia and bushwillow. Very bad tar④ deteriorated to intermittent strips of small stones and gravel, which is why there were plenty of roadworks with sandy detours. After Guija village, potholes peppered the tar left and right. Before crossing the Limpopo River we were stopped by a boom so that a toll of 10 meticais (MZN) could be exacted from us; Keith's Toyota Hilux, though, required 20 MZN (it's considered a pickup). Just shows; it pays to drive a Freelander.

Be prepared for a continuous string of rural subsistence villages, consisting of clay or woven-reed huts spilling out playful kids, pedestrians, bicycles, goats and cattle (which is why 50kph is the drill). School was in session in an open-air reed enclosure. Big plastic bags bulging with charcoal lined the road. The most common sight was women and children bearing 20-litre water containers – the most pressing need for these villagers right now.

The road surface dramatically improved after connecting up with the coastal EN1. Towards the coastal village of Quissico, where we got our first glimpse of the sublime turquoise waters of a coastal lake, Mozambique's tropical nature takes root. Dune-forest trees were green and glossy, and the long, curved, pipe-thin trunks of coconut palms appeared in greater and greater numbers till we were driving through palm-lined avenues. At Inharrime we watched ribbons of blue-green lake water, bleached sand and densely packed palms pass us by. But the villages themselves are a chaotic conglomeration of reed shanties and stalls that stretch on and on, seething with people and action and animation. The wares are strung up, spread out or gathered in rumpled heaps – everything from vegetables, fruit and basketry to splendidly coloured bras, formal long-sleeved shirts, garden equipment and plumbing accessories. Next came Piri-Piri Central (as Hirsh called it): row upon row of flaming piri-piri sauce⑤ in glass bottles lined up on wooden stands outside villages.

Evasive action – not getting zapped by the plethora of traffic cops and their cameras on the road – earned the boys their post-trip beers. Just before turning onto the N5/EN101 to Inhambane, we were stopped at a permanent police checkpoint and asked to show our

---

Mozambique's woodland
- Mopane (*Colospermum mopane*)
- Fever tree (*Acacia xanthophloea*)
- Black monkey-thorn (*A. burkei*)
- Umbrella-thorn (*A. tortilis*)
- Ankle- or brack-thorn (*A. robusta*)
- Large-leaved false-thorn (*Albizia versicolor*)
- Russet bushwillow (*Combretum hereroense*)
- Red bushwillow (*C. apiculatum*)
- Leadwood (*C. imberbe*)
- Jacket plum (*Pappea capensis*)
- Sicklebush (*Dichrostachys cinerea*)

vehicle importation permit and registration papers. The officers were courteous, friendly and, after chatting about where we were headed, flashed wide smiles and wished us a good trip.

After a stop-start passage through the pedestrian and traffic chaos of Inhambane, a cluster of lodge and resort signs directed us to Casa Barry. The last kilometre, along the Ponta da Barra (Barra Peninsula), was an obstacle course of pitted, humpy rock, then pure sand. (Well, we had to justify the 4x4 angle, didn't we?)

The experience
In all the villages we were struck by the utter disrepair of once-existent brick and mortar buildings – now windowless and falling apart, crumbling and decaying – ranged cheek by jowl with functioning spaza stores, stalls and open-air markets. Even where there are standing walls, the villagers seem to prefer unpacking their wares in doorways, across floors and over pavements. Relics of old colonial Portuguese architecture endure here and there, particularly tiny churches still with their painted blue-and-white tiles intact, carrying iconic images of Mary Magdalene. One word of advice: hold off on the coffee before setting out since there aren't many opportunities to pee, not even a discreet piddle behind a bush. Even the EN1 is highly populated along its entire length – and where there isn't a hut, there's a pedestrian. Or three.

... views through sighing casuarinas across long gentle ocean rollers

Relief does come in the form of the excellent Alcar Petromoc just north of Chidenguele. Modern and new, it has a little supermarket-style store stocked with all the essentials, a small food store, a café with pumping music, and absolutely spotless toilet facilities for 10 MZN, worth their weight in gold. (We did also spot a huge sign for toilets at a craft centre just south of Chidenguele but weren't brave enough to try it.)

Mode of abode
Casa Barry has a prime spot on the peninsula, which protrudes from the coastline like a small thumb. Standing on the edge of the powdery sands of Tofo Beach, ⑥ much touted in guidebooks, it also has the oddest situation in that two small tourist establishments have sprouted up in front of it, interrupting part of Casa Barry's shore frontage. The reed-walled, reed-thatched (locally known as *makuti*) units, beautifully crafted and in different sizes, are raised on stilts to maximise views through sighing casuarinas across long gentle ocean rollers. Ours (Casita C) definitely pipped the others for best vista. And we were seduced by the spacious thatched, wooden deck, where much of our time was spent relaxing at the giant wooden slab of a table, surf pounding in our ears. Inside is an airy, double-volume kitchenette (very well equipped); a sea-facing main suite with mosquito net, overhead fan and handcrafted wood-and-cane furniture; a second, darker, bedroom with similar facilities; and a modern toilet and shower cubicle.

DAYS 3 AND 4
Casa Barry, Tofo
The experience (terra firma)
We settled into the island lifestyle faster than ice melts in a glass in a heat wave. The beguiling curve of unspoilt sand and hissing surf lured us for early-morning runs to the lighthouse on the point. Across the dunes, reed beach lodges displayed

various levels of rustic: thatch segued from 'fringes' clipped and trimmed like a hedge to untamed and scruffy, akin to a long-haired terrier peering from behind a scraggly mane. From early morning on, local beach sellers ambled past, brandishing pineapples and pawpaws or the fresh catch of the day – prawns, calamari, crayfish or fish strung from a stick. Beach bars like Dino's drew us in for lunch. A coolly laid-back, brightly painted place with scraggly thatch, wooden benches, full-size Bob Marley woodcarving and loud music, Dino's wasn't going to win any prizes for its food, but the beers were cold.

Meals at Casa Barry were eaten at polished wood-slab tables on a huge outdoor deck with expansive views over the shoreline. Here the boys drank chilled Laurentinas[20] (judged nicer than the oft-touted 2M) and we savoured our first crunchy, fiery piri-piri prawns.

The experience (ocean depths)

The whale shark tally around Tofo is 629 – that's 18% of the world's population – and this is generally attributed to circular currents moving between Madagascar and the Mozambican coast which stimulate an upwelling of nutrients such as phyto- and zoo-plankton. This draws in whale sharks year round, whereas winters attract calving humpback whales. So we didn't need too much arm-twisting to sign up for an 'ocean safari' with Peri-Peri Divers (their slogan: the 'hottest' dives around). The rate of difficulty of their scuba dives varies from 'lemon and herb' or 'mild' to 'hot'. But we were going on safari.

A short video and briefing behind us, mask, snorkel and fins in hand, we all pushed and shoved the Rubber Duck into the shallows before clumsily clambering in. The skipper gunned the boat through cresting water into even bigger heaving swells – daunting walls of water that appeared insurmountable yet the vessel rode them with consummate ease.

We didn't have to venture too far out to sea before other dive boats alerted us to the presence of a whale shark. Overboard we went, trying to make as delicate a 'plop' as we could – a boatful of arms, legs, fins and snorkels makes this well nigh impossible – then adjusting our gaze to the watery depths and finning as hard and fast as possible to follow the moving shadow. Twice the dark shape loomed gigantic below me, white spots and coarse skin visible in the clear turquoise water. But the whale shark moves so fast you have to kick like hell – and contend with a raft of bubbles, thrashing fins and mouthfuls of hair from the snorkellers around you. Then there is much heaving and clambering and wrenching of arms almost out of their sockets to get you back into the boat for the next sighting. A few celebratory bruises are guaranteed.

... the dark shape loomed gigantic below me ...

Next up was a pod of common dolphins, tumbling and surfing around the boat; underwater I watched a trio practising vertical dives before they streaked away.

The afternoon was capped by the appearance of two sets of mother-and-calf humpback whales: first up, spout and spray, then a huge glistening curved back, like polished rock, rising slowly from the water, next, a large fin, and finally great tail flukes. We were enthralled.

The race in to shore⑦ kept our adrenaline pumping as we wedged our feet into boat straps and gripped ropes to ride tall waves – feeling as if we were airborne above the seething ocean – but again the buoyant vessel travelled easily across the foaming crests and we shot onto the beach, tumbling out, exhilarated.

DAYS 5, 6 AND 7

Casa Barry to Pomene Lodge, Pomene (200km)
Time it took us: 4½ hours

The drive

From Casa Barry, we retraced our route through a tight jostle of beach lodges, resorts and laden coconut palms on bad tar to Inhambane. The town is announced by a continuous string of informal reed structures to either side of the road – haphazard, untidy, chaotic – balancing offerings of every description. In spite of its position on Inhambane Bay, and its ageing promenade cradling the town, there is no beauty here to appreciate. A few once-beautiful Portuguese buildings, with Arab influences evident in arches and intricate stonework, stand jaded and unkempt, mould creeping in, paint peeling. In fact, it's the informal markets that bristle with sociability and energy and tumult. The red-and-white Vodacom livery emblazoned on every surviving wall – the clashing turquoise and yellow colours of Mozambique's M-Cel have a tough time competing – is what catches the architecturally starved eye.

The EN101 led us away, hooking us up with the EN1, which took us through little towns with names we've all heard – Maxixe, Morrumbene, Massinga – but with nothing much to commend them. After 2¾ hours on the road, a right turn to Pomene (well indicated, thereafter follow the signs) on sand became interesting; little did we know that the 40km to Pomene Lodge would take us 1¾ hours … 4x4-ers rejoice! Through jacket plum, acacia and palm trees, the vehicles tackled increasingly red sand, then bumped up and down humps and hills till the palms disappeared. Dune forest delineated the edges of the Pomene Nature Reserve, where, at the gate, we handed over 200 MZN per person and another 200 per vehicle. Soft sand increased,⑧ the *middelmannetjie* rose higher and the track became narrower, bumpier and more choked by dune vegetation. As we tracked the Ponta da Barra Falsa, a long spit that curves tightly in to ward off the restless ocean, the erect air roots of countless mangroves sketched a graphic landscape.

Before we'd even read the sign at 4.5km insisting that tyre pressure be reduced to 1.2 bars, the boys were out of their vehicles doing just that⑨; I watched, fascinated, while tiny fiddler crabs, one big claw totally out of proportion to the body, did a peculiar sideways scuttle among the mangrove roots.

Mode of abode

Pomene Lodge, part of Barra Resorts, has a stunning location on a long spit that has a saltwater lagoon and a mangrove wetland to one side, and wave-washed sugar-fine shoreline to the other. A string of wood-and-reed 'water chalets' on stilts, straight out of a Maldives brochure,

Know your central Mozambican palms

Coconut palm (*Cocos nucifera*)
Wild date palm (*Phoenix reclinata*)
Lala palm (*Hyphaene coriacea*)

Spotted at Pomene
Crowned Hornbill
Burchell's Coucal
Dark-capped Bulbul
Greater Flamingo⑪
Little Egret
Common Ringed Plover
Crab Plover
Whimbrel
Curlew Sandpiper
Sanderling

faces the ever-changing lagoon tides through sliding-glass doors. One minute the water is lapping at the edge of your deck, mangroves knee-deep in water, the next it has retreated into the distance leaving ridged sand and water rivulets strewn with white corals, shells and air roots. The cabana walls are intriguingly fashioned from bundles of reeds tied together, then bound side by side. The units are topped by *makuti* thatch, and a bushy fringe finishes it all off. There is much to like about the cabanas: airy double-height rooms hold a giant double bed swathed in mosquito netting; the attractive bathrooms are clad in wood; the furnishings are natural straw and wood; and plaited decorative details add lively interest.

The experience
The administration-bar-restaurant complex,⑩ pretty as it is with an elongated curving pool crossed by a handcrafted wooden bridge, left a tad to be desired. Yes, we were way out of season, the lodge was clearly operating on a skeleton staff and, being so remote, getting supplies in and out must generally be a major logistical challenge. But, off a menu of heavily meat-based offerings, the cooking was uninspiring. The crab

> **... leaving ridged sand and water rivulets strewn with white corals ...**

curry, one evening, bristled with potential. And yet … we were stared down by a giant-clawed carapace – only the beady eyes were missing – then handed a massive wooden pestle to crush our way through dinner. I passed.

And there is *no* excuse for bad coffee. Ricoffy just doesn't cut it.

On the first day, being the second of only two sets of guests, we were delivered into the capable but immensely laid-back hands of the one and only waiter, Gito, then left very much to our own devices. Beyond that, enthusiasm and a warm personal touch were in definite short supply.

And just a suggestion: some information on Pomene Nature Reserve's nine mangrove species, the plentiful water birds – we witnessed pink clouds of crimson-winged Greater Flamingoes – and scuttling mangrove crabs would score some kudos. Also, what would it take to have someone clean up the thin ribbons of plastic flying like celebratory streamers from the mangroves at the water chalets? Just saying …

Now that's off my chest, the setting truly is inspiring. We ate dinner (with the entire place to ourselves) under the stars with palms leaning conspiratorially overhead, water slapping a couple of metres away. More idyllic you don't get.

Old Hotel, Pomene
Don't leave the lodge without visiting this ruined complex – sprawling, windowless, graffiti-covered remains of a once-elegant Portuguese hotel, still sporting dangling red-clay roof tiles and even painted ceramic wall tiles. It's the spectacular position that takes your breath away: on one side, a hilltop panorama of lazy shallow waves, kilometres of blonde sand and a deserted curved cove, on the other, jagged black rocks where fishermen cast their lines and blowholes spout skyward as the sea crashes in. We explored the hill beneath the heavy, charcoal frown of a crackling electrical storm.⑬ Dramatic indeed.

DAYS 8 AND 9
Pomene to B D Lodge via Vilanculos and Inhassoro (324km)
Time it took us: 4 hours to Vilanculos

The drive
We retraced our sand-and-mangrove route back to the EN1, and headed north to Vilanculos. Just be diligent about the 60kph, sometimes 50kph, speed limits through an incessant string of villages. Around Mavanza and Nhachengue, marvel at the sudden appearance of grove upon grove of baobabs. In winter, leafless and strung with pendulous cream of tartar pods, they were just like wire trees decorated with Christmas baubles.

Where character is concerned, Vilanculos doesn't much excite: it's a blend of reed structures, crumbling edifices and brick-and-mortar buildings. Our only highlight was Kilimanjaro Café, located in a soulless little centre, where we had our first half-decent cup of coffee (cappuccino!) in a long, long while. We'd read that we should drop into Café Mozambicano to try its famous Portuguese custard tart, *pastel de nata*, but we were running out of time. We had a sea tide to beat …

After the Vilanculos turn-off, the EN1 was pitted and potholed, with some holes the size of small craters. With a right turn onto the R252 to Inhassoro, the 4x4s were down to a single lane of ragged-edged tar flanked by sand. Oncoming vehicles had us straddling tar and grit, then climbing back onto tar again. Just outside the Inhassoro village proper, a little wooden signpost for B D Lodge directed us onto a humpy-bumpy sand track filing behind a string of beach lodges till a second rickety sign pointed towards the beach route. There *is* a second road running parallel to the beach route but it runs through a tidal mangrove swamp and the sucking mud generally makes it impassable (hence the concession to drive on the beach).

The experience
(Note: throughout Mozambique driving on the beach is forbidden except for certain restricted-access sectors, for which a permit *must* first be obtained.) We had to carefully time this leg for low tide to ensure we had compacted sand to drive along and enough time before the incoming seas hemmed us in against the high dunes. The beach gradient here is even and flat for hundreds of metres out to sea, so once the tide rises it does so fast. We knew the 35km stretch would take us about 40 minutes with no stops. The tide was coming in, but we still had an hour or so to play with.

Permits in hand, we ground through a low barrier of churned-up soft sand to get onto the beach. The stormy sky settled in to fifty shades of blue and grey,[12] and the light was dramatic: dove-grey, eggshell-blue, steel-blue, shimmering zinc. The sea, mute and weakly green, was flat as a skillet. To our left, briefly, was a bit of dune forest with palms and banana groves. We bounced across a series of large sand ripples, slid through a deep sand patch, and crunched across dried seaweed strewn across the beach, liberating its pungent smell. Thereafter the sand was beautifully firm but for a few pliant patches.

Then, out of nowhere, sunbaked dune cliffs, riven by fissures and deeply eroded gullies, loomed 40m above us, badgering us onto a narrow zone of beach between a bulwark of dunes and the ocean. Kilometres of flat, untainted sand, scored only by two pairs of wheel tracks, unravelled ahead of us. It was a landscape containing the purest of lines, unmarred by any intrusion of wood or rock or crabs. So isolated, so deserted, so devoid of people, boats or civilisation. It was a marvel.[14]

PLEASE NOTE: beach driving **only with a permit**

The cliffs eventually subsided to white-sand dune hummocks crested with green scrub. The green-grey line separating sea from sky was interrupted at intervals only by the needle of a mast. Sometimes a solitary, weather-ravaged boat, fashioned out of planks of wood nailed together and bound with tyre strips and twine (and looking impossibly unseaworthy), was pulled up on the sand.

B D Lodge is at the end of a land spit, and as the point drew closer, the exit track off the beach became evident as a broad sandy entry, way into the dunes. It needed a firm foot and a steady throttle … it's very easy to get mired in the soft, powdery sand.

Mode of abode

I came close to loving B D Lodge (stands for Bartolomeu Dias, in a nod to nearby Dias Point) the most. The entire complex – rustic, but in a nicely appointed beach-house way – is utterly charming. ⑮ The sprawling main building of wood and reed – and soaring double-volume proportions – opens up along one side, by means of rows of folding wooden doors, onto a big deck with a pool and lounger chairs. On every other side big shutters swing up, held in place by chains, to let in the views and cooling breezes. The lodge is filled with lovely pieces of driftwood, giant wood-sculpted fish, woven baskets and carved wooden bowls cradling pretty shells and sea beans. At the bar, lengths of tree trunk sliced in half become tables and benches.

Beyond the deck, not 20m away, the sea rolls gently in. Following the wild storms of January 2012, the

… delectable pão rolls stuffed with garlic snails

lodge owners have started to build an enormous protective barrier in front of the main lodge using bags of sand, which will eventually become naturally shored up by the action of the incoming waves.

Sprinkled very discreetly among the vegetated dunes, thatched wooden cabins raised on poles are connected by winding paths lined with reed matting.

Gerry, Cassia, Carlos and Paulo were our gracious, involved, and eternally helpful hosts. Perhaps because it was out of season and we had the luxury of the entire lodge to ourselves the first night, Cassia was our personal chef. Platters of freshly caught couta and calamari constituted dinner one night, succulent giant crayfish the next. Hors d'oeuvres were the most delectable *pão* rolls, crusty on the outside, soft on the inside, and stuffed with garlic snails. Breakfast, too, was carefully and beautifully presented and served. It was all truly classy. (I can't speak for in-season, though, as reputedly it's filled with rum-and-Coke-swilling fishermen.)

Johnson's Beach Bar, Inhassoro

You probably have to ask the locals the way as the bleached wooden signboard won't help much. A tight sandy track, steep dips included, threads through dunes onto the beach. Here, a thatched bar structure with walls of acid-green, orange and purple sits under coconut palms. ⑯ You perch on wooden stools under thatch umbrellas and gaze at a calm waveless sea while drinking your Laurentina or 2M and snacking on hot, spicy prawns (piri-piri sauce compliments of the waiter's grandfather's trusted recipe). Rasta curio sellers add to the decidedly Caribbean air. It must pump in summer.

DAY 10
B D Lodge to Flamingo Bay Water Lodge, Barra Peninsula (396km)

The drive
It was time to start retracing our steps for home. Another exhilarating beach drive back to Inhassoro linked us up with the EN1, and it was straight down the coast back to the Barra Peninsula. Here we checked into Barra Resorts' Flamingo Bay Water Lodge for a night (*see* panel, this page).

DAY 11
Flamingo Bay Water Lodge to Sunset Beach Lodge, Chidenguele (233km)
Time it took us: 3 hours

The drive
The EN101 led us to the EN1, which took us south to Chidenguele. A signposted left turn to Chidenguele Beach is followed by signs to Sunset Beach Lodge. The bumpy sand road is punctured by successive humps and corrugations, finishing in a rise, then a steep bumpy dip. After you swing through the lodge gates the track becomes sandier and is briefly hemmed in by high earth banks.

Mode of abode
This brick-and-mortar complex (a change after all the reed and thatch) commands an unbelievably scenic spot on the crest of a hill⑱ with wraparound views on to the ocean, where low rollers slope quietly in. A low-slung main building, all mute greys, has maximised its frontage with split-level wooden decks, benches and umbrellas. There is a 6- to 10-person guesthouse, two self-catering casas – Casa 1 was ours – and camping facilities with private ablutions.

Our casa featured floor tiles, bamboo blinds and an airy kitchenette/lounge with trendy fittings and a long bar and bar stools (and extra bunk beds). The two bedrooms had lovely African-inspired embroidered linen and a modern toilet/shower. Outside, the verandah gave on to those stunning sea views.

Flamingo Bay Water Lodge
Pretty as a postcard from some exotic clime, 20 wooden water chalets stand on a crisscross of stilts⑰ over shallow crystal-clear waters, facing a mangrove-lined shore backed by coconut palms. Leading to them is a boardwalk so long, it feels as if you've hit Hotel California … once you're on it, you'll never get off (sorry, Eagles, for the mangled lyrics). *Makuti*-thatch roofs, white linen, pod-husk lampshades – it's exceptionally lovely. The main hotel, though, exudes a decidedly Southern Suns resortish ambience (it's Barra Resorts). And in spite of it being the end of winter, the place was heaving. With South Africans.

DAYS 12 AND 13
Sunset Beach Lodge to Massingir Dam (Aguia Pesqueira: 325km)/Giriyondo Border Post (57km)
Time it took us: 5 hours

From Chidenguele back to Massingir Dam we dodged potholes, as we retraced our original route into Mozambique. When we got to the dam, where we re-entered Limpopo

National Park to claim our reservations for Campismo Albufeira (and paying another set of park fees), things got interesting. We no longer had a reservation, even though we carried physical proof of the internet transaction. And the camp was full. Our protests were met with a shrug of the shoulders. Someone had definitely slipped someone else a South African blue note. Maintaining an even temper and wielding immense patience, Hirsh (he's the negotiator) was eventually given the option for us to stay in the park's fishing cabins at a second camp, Aguia Pesqueira (meaning 'fish eagle') – except that it was 25km away. Definitely a case of a surreptitious blue note.

The drive
What they didn't mention was the quality of the road … a 4x4 route of note, we discovered. Thanks to high clearance and rugged tyres, we bumped and slid and swayed over humps, gulleys, loose stones and wash-aways, the worst buffered by pebbles. Our vehicles forged through dense mopane woodland which became tree stumps which became russet sand. The last 5km were the most testing. Then we had to sign in with the camp guard.

The experience
This time the standoff took over an hour. The fee for Aguia Pesqueira was R100 more than for Albufeira. (Heaven alone knows why … the cabins were older and under-maintained, with a skeletal array of equipment. Paraffin lamps came sans fuel, although solar lighting saved the day.) We hadn't messed up; they had. And it simply went against our principles.

Hirsh is the one with the patience. It was Sunday and our cellphone calls elicited no response from managers or people in charge. The standoff endured till the camp guard realised how immovable the rock was that he was up against.

He handed us the keys. Our cabins, rudimentary though they were, had views through to the dam, and the regular refrain of fish eagles made our spirits soar.

The following day, the leg to the border surprised us with a brief encounter with five or six elephants, among them two young ones. Life on the Mozambican side of the park!

Then we were through Giriyondo, returning old forms, filling in new forms, no hassles. Politeness reigned. We were asked if we were taking anything into South Africa; a couple of depleted storage boxes were inspected, curiosity was satisfied. In no more than 30 minutes, we were back on Kruger soil.

Primed for our next adventure.

ATENÇÃO
TRAVESSIA DE ELEFANTES

ATTENTION
ELEPHANTS CROSSING